MAN Changes

WHAT YOU DO....

GAME Changes

WHAT YOU GET....

MAN Changes
WHAT YOU DO....
GAME Changes
WHAT YOU GET....

Authored By,

Passion Prasad

Disclaimer

Registered Office- 907-Sneh Nagar, Sapna Sangeeta Road, Agrasen Square, Indore – 452001 (M.P.), India

Website: http://www.wingspublication.com
Email: mybook@wingspublication.com

First Published by WINGS PUBLICATION 2024

Copyright © Passion Prasad

Title : MAN Changes, GAME Changes

Price : Rs. 799/- | $ 9.9 | AED 49

All Rights Reserved.
ISBN : 978-93-6006-571-3

LIMITS OF LIABILITY/DISCLAIMER OF WARRANTY

Blessed is the spot and the house, and the place, and the city, and the heart, and the mountain, and the refuge, and the cave, and the valley, and the land, and the sea, and the island, and the meadow where mention of God hath been made and His praise glorified.

~ Baha'u'llah

I am Happy. I am Healthy.
I am Powerful. I am Successful.
I am Positive. I am Passionate.
I am Rich. I am Abundance.
I am Energetic. I am Enthusiastic.
I am disciplined. I am Determined.
I am Focused. I am Fortunate.
I am Blessed. I am Blessed.
Affirmation Morning !!

PASSION PRASAD

Contents

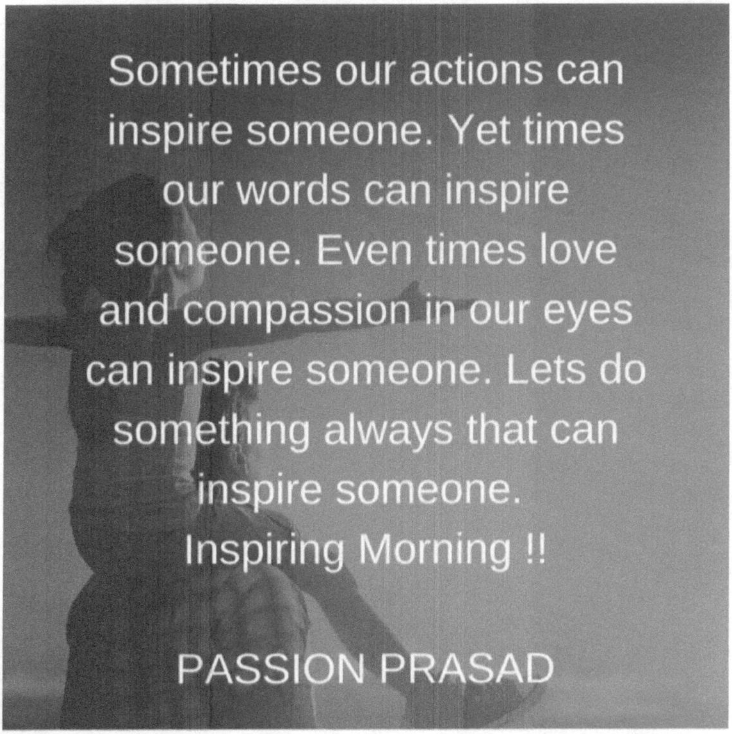

Sometimes our actions can inspire someone. Yet times our words can inspire someone. Even times love and compassion in our eyes can inspire someone. Lets do something always that can inspire someone.
Inspiring Morning !!

PASSION PRASAD

Dedication

I take this opportunity to express my deep love
and soul connection to my wife Li Chen and
I humbly honoured to dedicate this book to her for
her unconditional love and for her spiritual and
moral values. Without her relentless support,
this book would not have materialized.

Everyone has their own aura.
Every city has its own charm.
Every country has its own
culture. Every continent has
it's own beauty. Everything
has it's own features,
specifications, advantages
and benefits.
Everything is Unique Morning!!

PASSION PRASAD

Foreword

I have read several books and had opportunity to meet many highly accomplished and successful people in my life. This book is an essence, a summary and a result of my experiences, my thoughts, my intuitions, my observations and my perceptions. I hope this collage of thoughts, ideas and interpretations help the readers in enhancing their knowledge and enriching their lives. I pray that every soul on this earth may live happily, peacefully and purposefully.

I have been writing my personal motivational quotes since 2012 and sending them every morning to nearly two thousand people through different social media platforms. I create my own quotes based on my understanding, my perceptions and my observations. I love to observe each and every thing happening in and around me and try to learn something from everything. This gives me ample thoughts, ideas and intuitions for my daily morning quotes. I am glad and a little proud that I could consistently maintain sending those quotes for the past twelve years. Some of the recipients cherish them and store them in their computers or mobiles. A few of these quotes you may see in between the chapters here.

I have been fortunate to meet several highly intellectual people in my life. I am inspired by many stalwarts of this world. Some are still alive and some have left this planet.

To mention a few, I am inspired and motivated by the motivational coach Jim Rohn. He has inspired millions of people with his profound knowledge and wisdom and he narrates the principles in crystal clear way. I have watched several videos of his motivational talks on personal development and they have left deep impact on the growth of my mindset and thinking methodology. I salute his soul.

I also take this opportunity to give my reverence to Bob Proctor and Zig Ziglar. Their charisma, character and command over the subject are remarkable and very few souls of that calibre come to this beautiful planet.

I am deeply moved by the book "Think and Grow Rich" by Napoleon Hill. This book is a marvel even to this day, probably more so nearly a century after its first publication.

I have been fortunate to meet Dr Steven Covey, author of "7 Habits of Highly Effective People". He is a genius. His in-depth research and analysis of the human behaviour and mindset is exemplary. He has had a significant impact on my life.

I am also fortunate to have met Tony Robbins during his "Unleash the Power Within" program in London. How he started his life, how he has evolved and how he has grown is a phenomenal example of sheer determination, will power and focus. His famous quote "It's your decisions, not your conditions that determine your destiny" comes to my mind frequently.

I have been fortunate to meet Dr Deepak Chopra accidentally in San Francisco Airport. It was by pure coincidence that I met him due to a flight delay to San Diego. If the flight had been on time, I would have not met him. We had a good conversation and later I was fortunate to visit Chopra Foundation the next day to explore their activities and facilities.

We meet different people in our life not by accident, but by coincidence. If we can connect the dots, we can weave the story and can understand the logic, sequence and reasons behind every incident in our life.

I admire Robin Sharma, author of the book, "The Monk Who Sold His Ferrari" and many other several books including "The 5 AM Club". He is a simple but effective and emphatic thought creator. I attended one of his seminars in Hyderabad and I admire his authenticity, dedication and commitment to serve the world. I deeply honour him and pray that he continues to serve the world by sharing his wisdom and inspiration.

I have watched several videos of Les Brown. He is another genius with a never-ending flow of thoughts. I am amazed by his eloquence and wisdom. I salute him for his contributions to this world.

I have always believed that there are billions of people on this planet, but only a few will be remembered after they leave this planet. The difference is that those great souls have made a difference to society, communities, the world, and the whole planet.

Everyone lives their life. Taking birth, having education, getting a job, being married, buying a house, having children, buying a car, having assets and bank balance and in the end, leaving this world with empty hands. This is common to almost every human being on this planet, irrespective of their race, religion, region or reverence.

This is living life for us. Even though there are successes and struggles in this journey, but it is done by everyone. What is great about this?

Ultimately, what matters is what we do for others and what we contribute to this society, community or world. This does not mean that one should be wealthy to give donations or charity to others. This does not convey that at all.

At this juncture, it's worth remembering Mother Teresa. Everyone remembers her and respects her, right? Why? She selflessly served humanity with compassion, empathy and love.

Everyone also remembers Nelson Mandela; why? He showed humanity with empathy, peace and patience. He served his people.

Everyone also remembers Mahatma Gandhi, why?

He served his people selflessly with love and non-violence.

Such souls are rare, but will be revered and remembered for ages.

Inspiration comes from within.
Motivation is from external
factors. When motivation and
inspiration join together,
miracles happen and
innovations evolve.
Inspired Morning !!

PASSION PRASAD

Acknowledgement

I take this opportunity to acknowledge as much as possible to each and every one who has contributed me in writing this book. The first credit is to my Parents, Late T. Sadasiva Rao (My Father) and T. Chaya Devi (My Mother). Also, I acknowledge My Wife Li Chen for her continuous support, encouragement and inspiration. Additionally, I am thankful to my children Sears & Sharra for their love and affection.

Life is a journey. In this journey many wonderful souls enter our lives and we will have different experiences. But every experience teaches us lessons and leaves everlasting memories.

I am thankful to all my four sisters Vijaya Lakshmi (Jyothi), Jaya Lakshmi, Durga and Srilaxmi and their spouses Venkata Ramana, Srinivas Madiraju, Jayanth

Chennuri and Srinivas Somisetti respectively and their children for their warm love and deep connections.

I convey my special thanks to all our relatives from my wife's side Bala Ramasamy, Judy, Shehab, Tahereh, Late Li Tan and their kids. Thanks to my Malaysian friends Kavidas, Rajesh, Uncle Tina, Shri, Uncle Parviz and many others. Uncle Parviz is instrumental in helping me to proof read this book.

I convey my special thanks to Christina Fidel, Pastor, for all her guidance and wisdom. Special thanks to my friends Vikrant Prabhu, Lily, Pranav, Mamta, Raju Mohan, John Parocha, Florente, Vasista Bharagava Valluri, Amman, Sige, Sridhar Sampath, Arjun, Ramzi Rohani, Lalit Thakur, Vanessa, who stood with me through thick and thin with their unwavering support.

Some beautiful souls cross our paths in our lives. I would like to mention a few names like Nagireddy, Sardhak, Sumit, Romana, Vijay, Akhil, Shiv & Anju, Roshni & Pavan Mallaya and their daughter Adya, Edgar, Bhaskar & Chandini, Ronie, Hull Manju, Nisha Shivram, Ram Mohan Rai, Shruthi Kataria and many more. Also, I would like to appreciate Mr Khuram Shahzad (Khidmah) & Mr Imtiyaz (Khidmah). Khidmah is the Facility Management Company that looks after the facilities in our compound. They are doing a great job.

I acknowledge my thanks to our maid Durga & her husband Purna Bahadur for their dedicated service. While writing this book she is carrying and six months pregnant. Hope my book will be delivered before her delivery.

I do not know how to convey my love to our previous canine, Late Lucky and our present fur kids Skylar, Milar & Marvel. These innocent and pure creatures gave us immense joy, a purpose in life and an opportunity to serve. May God bless the whole animal kingdom.

There are many people who played a key role in my journey, but sometimes we may not remember all their names. I truly apologize if I have missed some of these names, but I am deeply grateful to each and every one of them.

If we have patience, every
problem has a solution. If no
patience, everything becomes
a problem. Where there is
patience, there is peace.
Where there is no patience,
there is chaos.
Patience Morning !!

PASSION PRASAD

Preface

This book "MAN Changes, GAME Changes" is a revolutionary and creative idea of the author on discovering the impact of daily rituals on the outcomes of key aspects of our life. There are many books on rituals, habits, leadership, money etc. which are also the chapters in this book. However, the author has developed the content in a different way and narrated the sequence with his eloquent thoughts and creative ideas.

This book is for everyone of all ages and for all around the world. Especially for those who are in authority, if they can read this book, it can give them some tips and techniques for better managing organizations and countries.

I hope readers will enjoy their journey of reading this book till the end and the author would love to know your comments and feedback via his email or other social media platforms.

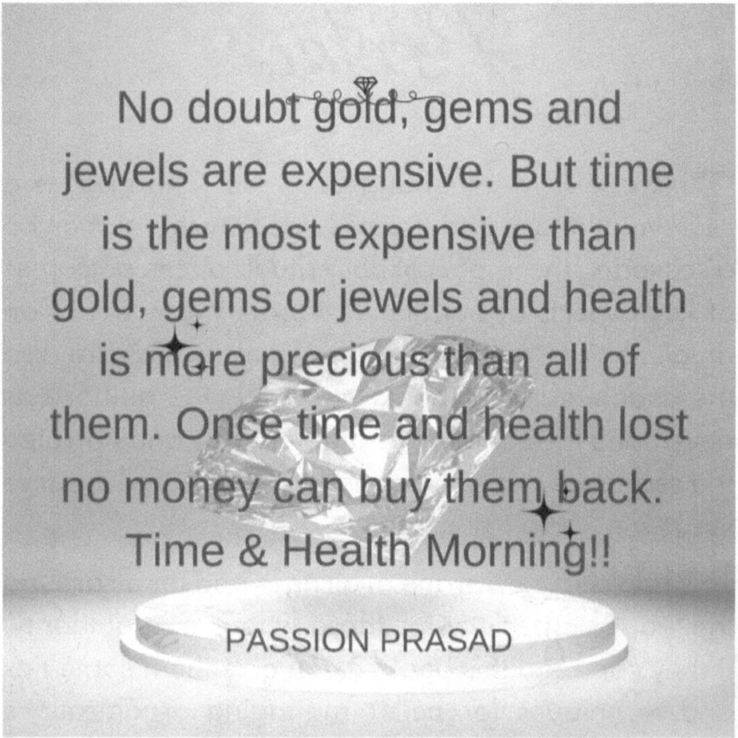

No doubt gold, gems and jewels are expensive. But time is the most expensive than gold, gems or jewels and health is more precious than all of them. Once time and health lost no money can buy them back. Time & Health Morning!!

PASSION PRASAD

Chapter 1

Man Changes, Game Changes

Introduction

The title of this book "MAN Changes, GAME Changes" is very self-explanatory. As man evolves his life evolves. As man changes his life changes. As man alters, his life alters. As man explores, life reciprocates. This is the essence of life on this earth ever since the beginning.

In fact, this is totally true. As the "Law of Attraction" states, man is the author of his life. Man is the creator of his destiny. Man is the master of his fate. I truly believe in this principle and have applied it practically and experienced magical manifestations in my life. This book is a perfect example of the manifestation of intentions. This proves the statement, "Thoughts become Things". Hence, anyone can do anything if one is determined and focused. "If I can do it, you can do it".

Everything is manifested twice in this world, first in the mind and next in this physical world. Television started as a thought in someone's mind, today it has become a reality. The computer started as a thought in someone's mind and today it has become a reality. The mobile phone has started as a thought in someone's mind and today it has become a reality. This book has started as a thought in my mind and today it has become a reality.

The Universe always blesses the person with strong determination, focus and hard work. If we are ready to pay the price, everything can be achieved. But here the price is not money. The Universe resonates with our energy. If we can match the energy of our intention and effort with the universe, nothing is impossible.

Life always throws challenges at us. Those who are aware and prepared can handle those challenges with courage and effectiveness.

Dreams bring defeats;
Dreams bring disappointments;
Dreams bring despair;
And then.....
Dreams bring determination;
Dreams bring dividends;
Dreams bring destiny;
Dreams bring distinction;
Dreams are everything.
Dream Big Morning !!

PASSION PRASAD

Chapter 2

Man Changes, Game Changes

A Paradigm Shift

Till now we have discussed that as a Man Changes, the Game changes. But there is a paradigm shift now. This is purely my thinking and I believe it is unique and creative. Now I will elaborate my concept behind these lines....

M stands for Morning

A stands for Afternoon

N stands for Night

(What You Do...)

This is the first part.

Now, the second part is

G stands for Goals

A stands for Achievements

M stands for Money

E stands for Energy

(What You Get...)

Now I hope you get a brief picture of MAN changes, GAME Changes. When what we do in the Morning, Afternoon & Night changes, our Goals change, our Achievements change, our Money status changes and our Energy levels change. Hope you are getting my point…

How to effectively change this Morning, Afternoon & Night (MAN)?

There are over a billion people on this planet. Everyone's Morning or Afternoon or Night is filled with something called Rituals. By changing our rituals, we can change our life, our destiny and everything.

I hope slowly you are getting the concept behind MAN Changes, GAME Changes. This is a revolutionary concept. If one can understand this concept clearly then his life can change dramatically.

In the following chapters, I will gradually decode this concept in depth. Please continue reading till the end.

Some people live a life of
abundance. Some people live a life
of turbulence. Some people live a
life of complacence.
Some people live a life of ignorance.

It's all in attitude and mindset.
The way we view things, the way we
live our life.
Abundance Morning !!

PASSION PRASAD

Chapter 3

Rituals

Rituals are nothing but a certain set of activities we do in everyday life. These rituals are mostly based on our habits. In a nutshell, ritual is a combination of few habits done together.

Now we need to write down what are the activities we do in everyday life. For example, everyday morning we wake up at a certain time, then brush our teeth, go to washroom, check our mobile, do some exercise or go for walking, eat our breakfast etc.

These activities change from person to person. It all starts from the time we wake up. Some are morning people; they love to wake up early. Their energy in the morning will be at a peak state.

Some are Afternoon people. They wake up a little late, but during the afternoon their energy levels are high.

Some are evening people, and their energy is high in the evening.

"A" which stands for afternoon which also includes evening rituals or if it is convenient for you. "N" which stands for night includes evening rituals as well. For convenience's sake, I chose Morning, Afternoon & Night (MAN).

Some are night people, and they put up late nights as their energy during that time is at its peak.

Irrespective of whether we are a morning person, afternoon person, evening person, or night person, we definitely have certain rituals.

My concept is that if we closely watch our rituals and make some adjustments and fine tuning, then we can change the direction of our life in a better way.

If we observe all successful people, they have a certain pattern of common rituals. They are disciplined and strictly follow their rituals at all odds. That's why they are successful.

If we are aware of this secret, everyone can be successful. Success is not one man's property. Success is in abundance, available everywhere for everyone. We just need to find the formula of success. That is all.

As mentioned, these rituals change from person to person, from place to place and from region to region. However, few rituals are common for every living person on this earth, irrespective of his position, profession, or power.

Flash Thought:

Do any of you have pets at home, either dogs or cats? Having pets is a blessing. I have two dogs at home. They are so lovely and loyal. They never see how much money we have in our pockets; they just see our love and shower all their unconditional love on us. They bring unity in the family. My wife and I may have arguments on several matters, but when it comes to the matter of pets, we are united. Their unconditional love keeps us always energetic and joyful. However stressed or frustrated we are, when we look at them, we smile, and joy comes back to us. Have pets and be joyful.

***

Man is a creature of habits. There is no one without habits. Whether he is a good person or bad person, rich or poor, black or white, short or tall, everyone has habits and some routine rituals.

If we can track the pattern of our habits and rituals, we are making the blueprint of our lives. **"Decode your rituals and create your destiny."**

These habits are not the same for everyone. Some drink coffee soon after they wake up. Some brush their teeth and drink coffee. Some do not drink coffee at all in the morning. This is a small example. But what we do is a repetition of these acts every day throughout our lives. This repetition of habits or activities or rituals is what decides our lives, health, moods, finances and relationships. Life is as simple as that.

Some habits produce good results in the long run and some habits deliver negative results in due course. That is why we should keep a close watch on our habits and decode them.

Some people go for a walk every morning. Over a period of time, they maintain good health, and their physical and mental conditions will become better. They stay healthy.Some people eat some sweets after their every meal. This is a small example, but over a period of time, their sugar levels go up and they need to go to a doctor. Then they have to take measures for reducing the sugar levels. We all know that prevention is better than cure, right? Then why don't we take preventive measures when it is in our own hands and interest?

Some people go for walking only after being prescribed by doctor. He or she knows that walking every day is good, isn't it so? But why they won't do it??

There can be several reasons why a person is not doing what is good to do. Of course, we have no right to comment on any individual's habits or choices or decisions. It's completely up to the individual.

But for discussion's sake, let us try to decode a few possible reasons.

Some people are not aware of what to do. This is lack of awareness. They need some education or knowledge or information or a course or something to know what and which acts are good to do.

Some people are aware of what to do, but they do not want to do due to laziness or some other reason. This is procrastination. They need someone to guide them in the right direction or they should realize that procrastination leads to destruction in the long run.

Some people are aware of what to do, but they are so busy with life that they do not have time to do so. They need time management. Time management is nothing but self-management. If we know what to prioritize, we always find time. If someone likes to watch movies, he will always find the time to watch movies. We allocate time to the activities we like to do. But the important thing is, are we allocating time to the activities which are supposed to be done whether we like them or not? This makes the difference between success and failure, good health and illness, being rich and being poor, being happy or being dull....

How to know which is a good habit or a bad habit? It's not a rocket science at all, isn't it? In everyday life, we watch several people doing different activities giving different results. We have people in our own family, neighbourhood, society, office. We can learn from other people.

For example, smoking is injurious to health. Everyone knows that. But why do people keep on smoking? I am not against people who smoke. Everyone can have some habits for relaxation, pleasure or to feel happy. But are they under control???

In my opinion, everything is okay if it is under

control; nothing is ok if it is out of control. This is my philosophy.

Secondly, we are fortunate to have internet with all the information and content on every topic available online, in this age. We can also refer to Google or some search website to find what is good and what is not. We can get all this information and details very easily now-a-days online.

Here is another good question. If a man has good habits, is he a good person? If a man has bad habits, is he a bad person??

This is a million-dollar question. We can't draw any fixed line on this topic. But let me give a piece of my mind on this.

There are some people with good habits and good thoughts and good deeds. Of course they will turn out to be good people.

There are some people with good habits, but somewhere in their thinking pattern or in some of their actions, there will be some misalignment. They will be far from being completely a good person.

There are a few people with few good habits and few bad habits. But they can turn out to be good or bad based on their mindset and actions.

There are some people with few bad habits, but they are very generous and compassionate. They help people and serve people. So bad habits doesn't mean a bad person..

"Habits are personal, but attitude is social." How's that???

Habits are purely personal. If they don't affect his social life, like his attitude, character, actions and interactions with other people, I guess it should be okay, right??

But if his attitude is bad, even if he has good habits, it doesn't make sense.

This is like putting perfume to cover some foul smell…

If his attitude is good, even if he has some bad habits, it's okay.

This is being transparent even with few cracks on the glass…

Now the question is how to get motivated to have good habits? The best possible answer from my side is to keep in the company of people with good habits. That will inspire you, motivate you and allow you to have good habits because of their association.

You must know the great saying, "If you tell me the names of five people with whom you spend your maximum time, we can predict the future of that person". It's absolutely true. Our company decides our destiny.

Most importantly, one should have good intentions and pure thoughts. If the intentions are pure & sincere and thoughts are genuine & focused on helping others selflessly, everything can happen and then the world becomes a better place. Good intentions and pure thoughts lead to good habits.

By having good habits, we will have good results in our lives. Good habits bring good health, happiness, good moods, good relationships, good finances and cheerfulness all around. We can see that in many families around us.

To decode the rituals, we need to list down the activities we do in a day. The following sheet will help to list down for further action.

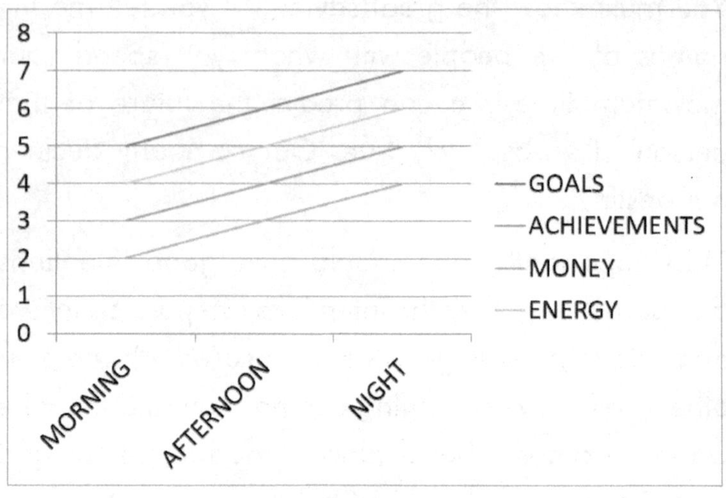
8
7
6
5
4
3
2
1
0
MORNING
AFTERNOON
NIGHT
GOALS
ACHIEVEMENTS
MONEY
ENERGY

M A N	TIME	ACTIVITY (LIST DOWN EACH AND EVERYTHING YOU DO EVERYDAY)	PURPOSE
MORNING		Wake up	
MORNING		How much time do I check my mobile	
MORNING		Exercise	
MORNING		Breakfast	
MORNING		Leaving for office	
MORNING		Quality moments with family	
MORNING		Leaving for office	
MORNING		Reaching office	
MORNING		What time I start my work	
MORNING		How many gtimes I do drink tea / coffee	
MORNING		How long do I work	
MORNING		How mhc nis my client time	
MORNING		How much is mobile / social media time	
MORNING		How much is my travel time	
MORNING		How much time for learning	
MORNING			
MORNING			
MORNING			
MORNING			

This sheet may look silly or simple,
but highly impactful for GAME in Life.

M A N	TIME	ACTIVITY (LIST DOWN EACH AND EVERYTHING YOU DO EVERYDAY)	PURPOSE
AFTERNOON		What time do I eat my lunch	
AFTERNOON		Do I drink water of anything else before my lunch	
AFTERNOON		Do I eat home cooked foor or outside	
AFTERNOON			
AFTERNOON			
AFTERNOON			
AFTERNOON			
AFTERNOON			
AFTERNOON			
AFTERNOON			
AFTERNOON			
AFTERNOON			
AFTERNOON			
AFTERNOON			
AFTERNOON			
AFTERNOON			
AFTERNOON			
AFTERNOON			

This sheet may look silly or simple, but highly impactful for GAME in Life.

M A N	TIME	ACTIVITY (LIST DOWN EACH AND EVERYTHING YOU DO EVERYDAY)	PURPOSE
NIGHT		What time are you back from work?	
NIGHT		Do you drink coffee/tea in the evening or night?	
NIGHT		Do you go for evening walk?	
NIGHT		Do you go to gym?	
NIGHT			
NIGHT		Do you have parties everyday?	
NIGHT		Do you cook?	
NIGHT		Do you invite friends frequently?	
NIGHT		Do you read books?	
NIGHT		Do you play with kids?	
NIGHT		Do you have family dinner together?	
NIGHT		how much time you use mobile?	
NIGHT		How much you use laptop?	
NIGHT		how much time younwatch TV?	
NIGHT		What do you do before going to sleep?	
NIGHT		Whatb time you sleep?	
NIGHT			
NIGHT			
NIGHT			

This sheet may look silly or simple, but highly impactful for GAME in Life.

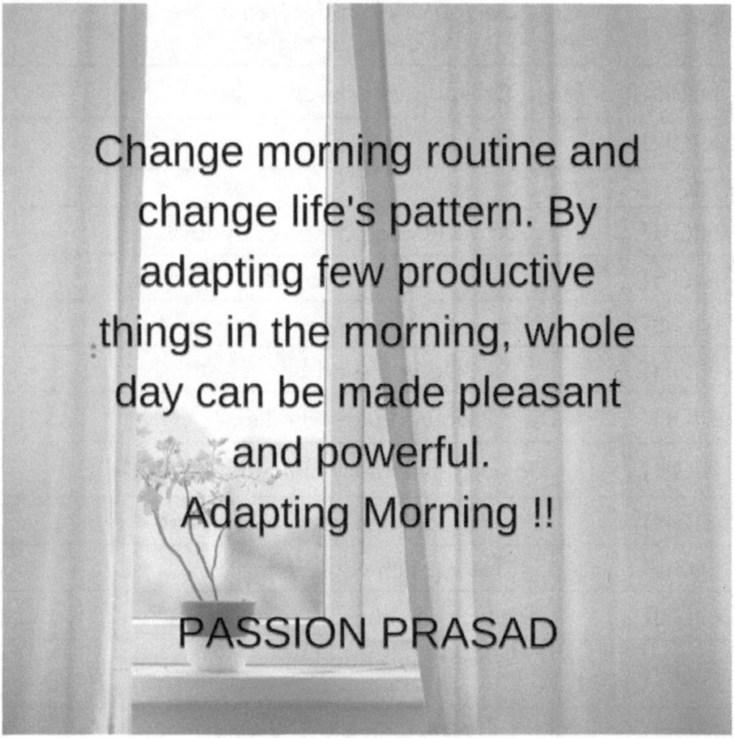

Change morning routine and change life's pattern. By adapting few productive things in the morning, whole day can be made pleasant and powerful.
Adapting Morning !!

PASSION PRASAD

Chapter 4

Best Practices

We all know the term ISO Standards. These standards are same internationally. In similar way, best practices are tried and tested methods or mechanism or measures or suggestions to do a particular task or thing or activity in a prescribed manner. These Best Practices normally doesn't change from region to region. There will be some deviations in certain critical conditions. Otherwise, best practices are the best practices anywhere and everywhere and are timeless.

Even in life, there are certain habits or activities or rituals which need to be done only in a certain way and that perfect way is called the best practice. For example, if we meet a stranger or a new person, we need to greet him with respect. This is a universal custom and this is a best practice.

If a person helps us in any way, we should say "Thank you" from the bottom of our hearts. This is a best practice.

If someone is in any need of help, we should try our best possible to help that person. This is a best practice.

This way, in every action or activity we do, there are right ways to do it and they are called the best practices. There are wrong ways and other ways too…

If someone is talking to us, we should pay complete attention and listen to their version without interruption. This is a best practice.

If we observe what people are doing sometimes we can feel that they are not doing the right way. That means they are not following the best practices. Sometimes we ourselves don't do things right way and that means we are not following the best practices at that time.

Best Practices are like the North Star. We should always direct our gaze towards the North Star. Then we are in the right direction in our life. If we don't follow the best practices that means we are away from the North Star and that implies we are not in the right direction and not aligned to the best standards of living.

Everyone wants to reach the right destination, right? When we follow GPS, we exactly arrive at the right destination precisely. Same way in life, we need to follow best practices to reach the right destination or to get the right results. That's it.

If someone wants to be a good athlete and if he doesn't get up in the morning and practice his routine, he is not aligned with his goal. That means he is not following the best practices.

When you join a company, there will be an SOP booklet accessible to everyone. SOP stands for Standard Operational Procedures. That means for every transaction or every operation we need to follow SOP's stipulated by the company. These SOPs are derived after thorough research, trial & error and after many discussions & negotiations. These SOPs are best practices for that company and everyone has to adhere to those rules.

Respecting parents is a best practice.

Respecting elders is a best practice.

I would just like to give a brief summary of some happenings in my life. I am a self-made man. After I did my engineering in electrical & electronics, I took a sales job at a computer hardware company. I joined before my engineering results came out as I wanted some pocket money, and I didn't want to depend on my parents. I don't know why I took that decision, but my career continued in sales & marketing for a long time. I started my life in a village, then moved to a town, then to a city, then to a metropolitan city, and then went abroad.

I somehow feel some of my daily rituals helped me to climb up the ladder in my career and life. Praying every day is one of my rituals. Praying refreshes our mind and body. Prayers attract blessings and can do wonders in life.

I worked in several countries like India, Saudi Arabia, Malaysia, Qatar, Dubai and Abu Dhabi. I travelled to more than thirty countries so far. I am mentioning this to emphasize that somehow and somewhere my daily rituals have helped me to explore the world. My rituals helped me to achieve my goals, achieve some significant milestones in my life, helped me in my financial platform and my energy levels.

My simple name is Prasad. When I joined toastmasters, people saw passion in my speeches and started calling me "Passion Prasad" and it has become my nickname. Now I am known as Passion Prasad to the world around me.

After few years, I went to the UK & the USA to attend several courses to upgrade myself and to find my passion. Later I quit my sales & marketing managerial job to follow my passion. I became a soft skills trainer and a motivational speaker. I gave several workshops, seminars and addressed thousands of audience to inspire them, motivate them and help them to find their passion in their life.

My life was not a smooth journey. I too had ups and downs. But somehow my rituals helped me to face the life's challenges boldly and come out successfully. This has inspired me to write this book "MAN Changes, GAME Changes". Our rituals make our life. I strongly believe that.

In life, every day will not be the same. Some days our energy levels are high and some days we find the bottom in our energy level and spirits. But our daily rituals can give us balance and help us to overcome such obstacles.

God has been very kind and merciful to me at every juncture of my life. He has guided me, protected me, uplifted me and saved me and has been very generous to me. I am thankful to the Almighty God for all his blessings on me and my family.

To mention some of my best practices or rituals that helped me in my life:

I pray every day, even while walking or doing anything and everything. Prayer is my everyday ritual.

Walking every morning has become my ritual. However, on a morning walk, one should follow certain precautions. During Corona, I used to walk 10 km in the morning and 10 km in the evening as there is not much to do during Covid time. I walked for more than 4000 km in a few months. I gave a speech, "Journey of one thousand miles" based on my walking experience.

But something happened after that. Once life had become normal after Covid, I went to play tennis after a long gap. I used to play tennis very frequently before Covid. But this time, when I started playing, suddenly, my ligament ruptured, and my leg became my handicap. The reason is too much walking will weaken our muscles. There should be always a balance in our activities.

The reason for telling this episode of my life is that I had to go for surgery for my ligament, and it stopped my tennis life. Once we undergo surgery, it becomes second-hand. It cannot be the same as before. So, we should always try to have a balance in whatever we do.

Build muscles, have proper diet, have good sleep. In everyday life there should be time for physical exercise, learning and personal development, good nutrition, some entertainment, good relaxation and most importantly good family time. After all, your family is the one who stands and walks with you all your life. A sound family leads to sound life.

We have two dogs, Skylar and Milar. Skylar is the mother and Milar is her daughter. I take them for walk 3 or 4 times every day. One of my best rituals is that I get up at 5 am everyday morning. That has helped me a lot in my life. I am a morning person. I accomplish many things before the world tries to wake up.

I believe those who wake up early in the morning will have a smooth, strong and successful life. I do not say that those who wake up late will not be successful. But if you observe the pattern of highly successful people and normal people, waking up early in the morning brings more success. Those who wake up late may be successful, but that may not last long, and they may lack something in life. That will make life incomplete.

Another good ritual I started a few years back is cooking. Cooking makes you more organized and brings more enthusiasm in life. Please try cooking if you haven't tried so far. And also, you can enjoy new dishes every day. Cooking brings creativity and it gives you more energy and motivation as well.

Especially when we invite our friends and cook for them, that will bring utmost satisfaction and happiness.

Everything depends on "Feel Good" Factor. When you feel good, you feel happy, you feel healthy, you feel energetic, you feel motivated and that will improve your interactions with others and will improve your relationships with others. Always try to feel good.

Here is my question: Why do you do what you do? You do anything and everything to feel good. If you buy ice cream for your child, she feels happy, and in turn, you feel happy. If you go out for a date with your spouse, that makes her feel happy, and in turn, you feel happy. If you cook for others, they feel happy, and in turn, you feel happy. When you go for a morning walk, you feel happy. The feel good factor is most vital, essential, crucial and special in everyone's life. Do anything and everything to feel good.

<u>Flash Thought</u>:

While writing this page, I just looked out through my window and could see the traffic light on the street. When the red light came on, all cars stopped. When the green light came on, all cars started moving again. Even so, in life, we often have red signals (struggles/challenges) and green signals (peaceful/joyful moments). When there is a challenge (red signal), just calm down and pause life for a while because soon, challenges will be solved, and a green signal will come on. We need to follow this signal paradigm to live a successful life.

Learn everyday from everything that happens, everything we see, everything we read and everything we watch. Learning is one skill we can do in every minute of our life that enhances our knowledge, skills and wisdom. Living is for learning and it's a never ending activity like breathing till the end. Learning & Development Morning!!

PASSION PRASAD

Chapter 5

Leadership

What is Leadership? There are thousands of definitions on Leadership by several great people in history. There are volumes of explanations available in the libraries and online.

In my opinion, if one strives to help other people & organizations and focuses on human capital development & material benefits (for companies) keeping aside one's selfish interest, that is true leadership.

Leadership is an attitude.

Leadership is an initiative.

Leadership is an influence.

Leadership is a mindset.

Leadership is a discipline.

Leadership is an approach.

Leadership is a habit.

Leadership is a quality.

Leadership is a philosophy.

Leadership is a nature.

Leadership is a vision.

Leadership is abundance.

Leadership is being authentic.

Everyone can be a leader. Robin Sharma, in his book "The Leader Who Had No Title" clearly states that anyone and everyone can be a leader. Leader need not be a CEO of a company or a person in power or someone with authority.

Even an ordinary house cleaner can be a leader. Even a taxi driver can be a leader. Even a barista in a restaurant can be a leader. Even the sales girl in a shop can be a leader.

The other day I was going for my morning walk. It was very humid and I was sweating like anything. We have garbage cleaners in UAE wearing green uniform and with a green garbage bin collecting the cans and stuff on the roads. Suddenly one garbage collector came to me and offered me a bottle of water. What a kind gesture!! I was totally amazed at his initiative to offer me a water bottle. That shows his compassion towards another human being. That is a kind of leadership.

There are many good people on this planet. Many are silent workers. They do good things silently and they do not look for appreciation or publicity. They just do because they want to do it. It is in their DNA. It's their nature. It's their attitude. It's their philosophy. There are many such people and we can see few such people in our everyday life. They are silent leaders.

Whenever we talk of Leadership, the names that come to our mind are Nelson Mandela, Mahatma Gandhi, Abraham Lincoln, Mother Teresa and many more. These great souls carved a niche in the annals of history. Their names remain there forever. They are leaders for the whole world.

There are many others whose names we will never find in newspapers or books or on any social media. The world is still going good because of these silent leaders. They just do it.

Flash Thought :

There are billions of people on this planet. Most of us went to school. In our text books we read the biographies or stories of Mahatma Gandhi, Abraham Lincoln or Nelson Mandela or Shakespeare. My question is, do you think anyone will read your story or my story in the text books???

Of course, there is very little chance for that. Why?? Because we are busy and caught up in living our life, building a house, getting married, buying car and building assets. But those people who are in the text books lived for the welfare, progress and growth of other people sacrificing their life and interests. That's why their names are in the history and our names are just on the name plate in front of our house.

When you live for others, you leave a legacy. When you live for others, the world salutes you.

***

<u>Flash Thought:</u>

When I go for my morning walks I keep 5 or 10, AED (Equivalent to 2 or 3 USD) in my pocket. Whenever I see workers on the way I just give them 5 or 10 AED. This is a small amount. But for them it is big as their salaries are very low. When you see joy on their faces it brings us immense joy. It brings us blessings as well.

LEADERSHIP continued…

Leadership is an internal attitude. In general, we are externally tailor-made men. We are barber made men. We are cosmetic made men. Our external appearance is completely designed to appeal to others or to please others. It's in my opinion, superficial.

But our internal world is completely different. We are internally thought made men. Our mind is the master director of our body, our attitudes and our external behaviour. Mind is nothing but our thoughts. True leadership emerges from our thought world. Leadership can be learnt, can be developed, can be improved, can be groomed and can be evolved. But leadership in its entirety emanates from the internal world.

Outside we may be wearing an expensive suit and costly gadgets and ornaments. This matters only to a small extent. What matters most is our internal thought processing. We will be rejected if our attitude is not good, even if we are in adorable attire. But we will be respected if our attitude is good, even if we are in simple and inexpensive attire.

Leadership is, in my opinion, a thought process. If our

internal thought process doesn't match our external behaviour, it's not true leadership. Leaders are transparent. They speak from their heart. If someone speaks through their mind, it's manipulative. Heart speaks truth, whereas the mind speaks altered thoughts. The mind is a machine that can interpret things differently and manipulate things and thoughts. But the heart translates and expresses thoughts genuinely, transparently and wholeheartedly. That's why when people try to confess, they say wholeheartedly, "I am sorry with all my heart". They never say whole-mindedly, "I am sorry with my entire mind".

Hope you are getting my point on mind and heart. No doubt mind is the master controller and generator of all our thoughts. But when heart is not aligned with mind, things go differently. But if mind & heart are aligned and in full synchronicity things will be genuine, pure, sincere, transparent, selfless, effective, efficient and energetic.

As you all know we are nothing but a reflection of our internal world. We are the face of our internal world. We are the representatives of our internal world. We are the ambassadors of our internal world. As the saying goes, Face is the index of man. Face is the index of our internal world.

Imagine even if we don't speak anything (not even a single word), people start making different impressions on us. When we speak the impressions will be confirmed. We reveal ourselves through our body language, nonverbal communication, eye contact and our gestures. So, people can get a brief picture of us even when we don't speak. How is it possible? Every part of our body, every cell of our body, resonates with what we are inside. They give signals to the outer world.

We as humans are both receivers and transmitters. We transmit our thoughts to the universe and we receive ideas from the universe. Our whole body is an antenna that can transmit and receive signals. We are highly sophisticated machines that can perform very unusual and hi-tech operations even without us being aware.

Our mind has connection with the Universe. Whatever we think it will be transmitted to the Universe. Universe knows our intentions. And our mind can receive signals from the Universe. That's why we get creative ideas, innovative thoughts and sixth sense feelings.

That's why I feel prayers are powerful. When we say prayers for our loved ones, even though they are sea miles away, our prayers reach them. The Universe works like a Satellite. It receives our prayers and transmits to our loved ones in the form of blessings. That means prayers are converted to blessings with a divine touch.

If we have good thoughts, they will be resonated and reciprocated accordingly. If we have bad thoughts, they will resonate and be reflected accordingly. That's why we should always have good intentions, good thoughts and good deeds. When they are in synchrony, we get blessings. The formula is:

Good intentions + Good thoughts + Good deeds=Blessings

The opposite is also true.

Bad intentions + Bad thoughts + Bad deeds = Curses

Whether it is blessings or curses, they are generated from us internally. That's why we create our destiny. Our karma is our destiny.

Universe never punishes us. We punish ourselves. We attract blessings or curses with our karma or deeds. If someone is blessed, it's because of their karma. If someone is cursed, it's because of their karma. It's as simple as that.

There is no heaven or hell outside. We create heaven or hell inside our own world through our karma or deeds. We can feel heaven or hell here itself. No need to wait till we die. Heaven and hell are here with us right at this moment, whether you agree or not. This is my belief.

God is there, but can we see Him? Does God exist? Well, that's another topic that cannot be discussed or explained here. Different religions and different theories are interpreted in different ways. But my understanding is that God is a belief. God is faith. God is energy. God is confidence. God is an unseen, unknown power that runs the world. If we believe in God, we can do miracles with faith and firm belief, only when we believe it.

We have seen many miracles in the lives of many other people on this planet. That's because of their belief, faith, trust and confidence. These are the qualities than can produce miracles.

Do you invest in yourself for personal development? Do you invest time to improve yourself?

Leaders always take time to improve themselves, polish their skills and improvise their persona. Leadership is like going to a gym. Day by day, the muscles grow and leadership also grows day by day. With every encounter, every experience, by solving every challenge, leaders evolve to become better versions of themselves.

When someone wants to be a champion in his particular field, he has to spend time and effort in the field of his passion for a number of hours. Someone said it takes a minimum of 10,000 hours of hard work to become the best in that particular game or art or craft. The more time and effort you spend on the field of your zone, the more you will become an expert. Even leadership is like that. But leadership is a 24-hour attitude. One cannot say I will be a leader only at work or only at some place. Leadership is a quality that you can use 24 hours a day. This is inherent and visible in every act we do. It doesn't show only in one area, but it's everywhere. Leadership is like the oxygen we breathe. It's there all the time, 24 hours a day.

Sometimes we find few people who are different externally and they don't live the same internally.

They don't walk the talk. They are not true leaders. There is a huge difference between a leader and a manager. Leaders walk the talk, initiate, coordinate and synergize to orchestrate the vision together whereas managers get things done by any means which can include manipulation and other methods.

Every manager cannot be a leader, but every leader is a good manager and beyond.

I met several high-profile leaders and high-profile managers in my life. When you meet them, you can feel whether they are leaders or managers. Leadership you can see in their eyes and gestures whereas for managers, you can see in their words and authority.

Leadership is not authority, it is authenticity.

Leadership is pure and crystal clear.

Leadership is like an ocean.

Leadership is abundance.

Leadership is a flow. Managing is a flow chart. There's a difference between flow and flow chart. Flow moves against any odds, but flow chart has many terms and conditions, if's and but's.

Leadership is like a symphony. Management is like boxing.

Leadership tries to win-win. Managers try to achieve win-lose.

I am not undermining managers at all. Everyone can check and self-assess whether they are just managers or true leaders. Managers are good, but they have limitations. True leadership is infinite with abundance.

Where a safety pin can solve the problem, you don't need a knife or a sword. In my opinion, managers use sword or knife everywhere irrespective of the size of the problem, but leaders are wise to use their tools to handle it better. They rarely use knife, but get things done with safe and simple methods.

I read somewhere, "Love is enough to get things done, but power is required to show only authority". This is absolutely true.

Are you adding value to others? Are you beneficial to others? Are you of service to others? Are you assisting others to live a better life with more comfort with your service and effort? Are you selfless? Are you committed? Are you sincere? Are you available? Are you affordable? Are you easily accessible?

These questions help us to understand whether we are leaders or not. Check out.....

I like the book "7 Habits of Highly Effective People" by Dr Steven Covey. I just would like to mention these 7 habits below:

1.   Be Proactive

2.   Begin with the end in mind

3.   Put First Things First

4.   Think Win-Win

5.   Seek first to understand and then to be understood

6.   Synergize

7.   Sharpen the saw

This is a profound theory to be effective and efficient in life, career and everywhere.

<u>**Flash Thought:**</u>

There is plenty of talent available in the world at present, which we have never seen before. Especially when we see the TV episodes like "America got talent" or "India got talent" or "Britain got talent" shows, we will be astonished and mesmerized by the skills they exhibit. Whether it is singing, dancing, painting, magic, or any other art or game, there are extremely talented geniuses there. That's the greatness of this modern era.

Especially if we look at films, whether they are Hollywood, Bollywood or Korean movies, there's plenty of creativity and technological wonders there. Actually, I was against movies. I used to think that they were like games played by rich people to rob money from ordinary people. But later, when I looked at it from a broader sense, I changed my opinion. Films are a platform to showcase your talents. Whether it is actors, musicians, cameramen, or technicians behind the screen, there's plenty of opportunity and creativity to showcase their skills and talents. And moreover, the film field is providing opportunities to thousands and thousands of people with employment. Now, I changed my opinion. Whether I watch it or not, the film field is not bad. It's giving livelihood to millions of people and entertaining people around the world and inspiring people (sometimes) to achieve the impossible.

Artists, whether through their singing or dancing or acrobatics, bring tears to our eyes. They make impossible things possible. How can this happen? Sometimes, in films, it is the photogenic effect or after taking several shots. But in Reality shows, it is live and on the spot. It's breathtaking and nerve-breaking. I salute those great geniuses. Some are born with talents and can perform even at very early stages of their childhood. Some learn, develop, improve and perform at the youth stage. But they are all truly brilliant. I am sometimes jealous of those prodigies… to be frank…

***

Flash Thought:

I reside in UAE. I wanted to finish my writing journey in 30 days. Here, summer is at its peak now in the month of July. The temperature is 45 degrees Celsius. Last week, I could not write my book as I was hospitalized for 2 days due to a heat stroke. Doctors said I was dehydrated and they put me on drip. I was there for nearly 2 days, and they gave me around 6 bottles of fluids. I am just informing that, in summer, we are supposed to drink lots and lots of water. It is suggested that we add some pinch of salt and a pinch of bicarbonate soda to water, which works like an electrolyte. Please drink lots of water in any season, especially in summer, to avoid heat strokes and dehydration....

***

The importance of education is enormous. Education is essential for growth and for personal development. Lack of education deprives many things in life. We see some labour working on the streets and at construction sites. They work for several hours every day under the hot sun, but they are paid very meagre wages. If they had been educated, they would not have been in such a state. I am not undermining labour and their valuable services, but I just want to reveal the fact for which they are in that state.

Those who are educated will be working in offices with higher salaries. In general, the more you are educated the more you are paid. The less educated are paid less. The importance of learning and development is the main essence of education. Education makes one eligible for better standards of living, better lifestyle and better earnings.

There are exceptions. Some who are not educated have become millionaires and billionaires. I am not talking about them. They are talented, privileged and fortunate to reach higher stages. But in general, lack of education deprives many benefits, advantages and privileges in life.

Education is of prime importance in life. Education is essential for both men and women. Men and women are equal in society. Boys and girls should go to school and enhance their knowledge, skills and talents. Girl education is more important as they will be the future mothers and they can educate and take good care of their children and entire family.

Education is learning, and learning is a continuous process. It never ends. Some may think that after getting a degree, education stops. Graduation is just a milestone in the journey of education. That is just to make one eligible to get a job for livelihood. But they should pursue their learning forever. That's why some people are promoted to higher positions because they acquired additional qualifications or accomplished additional courses in their respective field.

Let us take the example of the labourers who work very hard. After few years they may gain some experience, but their wages cannot grow drastically. There can be small increments, but not substantial. The point I want to emphasize is that education is essential. Education enables one to go higher and experience enables one to be on the top.

Every country, every religion and every culture should promote education for both boys and girls equally. If any country or religion deprives children of education, then it can be considered a crime.

There is a vast difference between blue collar workers and white-collar employees. The earnings of both categories are extremely different, their lifestyles are different, their assets are different and their bank balances are different. Their family status is different.

The more one focuses on getting education at younger age, the higher he goes in his later stage. Less focus on education will not take anyone higher. There are some people who focused on sports instead of education and that is perfectly okay. They focused on their passion. Pursuing passion is also a form of education.

For example, consider sportsmen like Lionel Messi. He has no big education, but he has skill at his hand,

and he has mastered it. Now he is paid very high. If one can pursue their passion in an absolutely professional way, they can definitely excel in their life. Otherwise, education alone can provide such benefits or heights.

In a nutshell, one should either pursue education or pursue their passion. Both can make them shine. If both are there, it's like icing on the cake.

But if there is no education and no passion, then it is devastation. Every parent should make sure that their children get an education, or they should pursue their passions seriously. Otherwise, they will be spoiling their children's future.

The people who spend hours and hours in library learn more and enhance their knowledge and wisdom. They go for research and doctorate and they flourish in their life.

Those who spend hours and hours in the field playing some kind of sports enhance their skills, talents and they definitely rise higher in their life.

Those who do not do the above both things either proper education or training in sports, will eventually be deprived of many things in their later life.

History has many examples of athletes who were successful in their life and also scholars who flourished in their life.

History also has examples of a few gangsters, thieves, robbers, etc. These people went in the wrong direction right from a young age. They probably had no education. They have not gone in the direction of their passion. It can be wrong guidance from their peers, or friendships with wrong people or association with evil groups. These things lead them to be in the wrong place, and in the end, they end up in prisons or being punished behind bars or sentenced to life. Where did things go wrong?

It can be because they didn't focus on their education when they were young. It can be because they didn't pursue their passion when they were young. It can be because their parents have not taken good care of them when they were young. All these factors lead them to land in wrong places. Can it be avoided?

Certainly!! By providing proper education at right age, such things can be avoided completely. Poverty can be one of the reasons for not getting educated. That's why every government should offer free education for all children so that no child goes uneducated and he or she will not go in the wrong direction. Such measures can eliminate crime in the society resulting in no thieves, no robberies and no gangsters.

If there is no free education, indirectly, this promotes crime in the society. Every government should realize this fact and take measures accordingly. If there is no free education and if every child doesn't pursue education, crime will increase, and there will be safety and security issues in society. We can prevent this by coming together. Education is essential for peace in society, countries, and the world. Lack of education is a danger to society, the country and the world.

Flash Thought:

Whenever summer comes, I make it a practice to keep some water bottles in my car and whenever I pass by some labourers or workers on the street, I give them water bottles. This is a simple act. But when we see joy and happiness in their faces, it brings us immense joy. This is a small ritual.

Leaders get things done by
keeping their people at ease.
Dictators get things done by
keeping their people at seize.
Leadership is an art,
Dictatorship is a threat.
Leading Morning !!

PASSION PRASAD

Chapter 6

Happiness

ife is simple. Success is simple. Happiness is simple. But we make life complicated, success complex and happiness confused with our thoughts. This may be due to lack of awareness, or no proper education or lack of learning or training and no proper guidance.

When you see a happy person you can feel it. Happiness is contagious. You cannot hide happiness. You cannot keep happiness with you alone. Happiness spreads like fragrance. When you put perfume to your body even surrounding people can smell it. Same way happiness can be felt by the people around.

Happiness is defined in several ways by different people. In my opinion, true happiness is when you do something to make others happy selflessly..

I read somewhere that money and happiness are like butterflies. If we chase a butterfly, we can never catch it. But if we patiently wait, the butterfly will come and sit on our shoulders. Money and happiness are like that.

In this modern world, people chase for money. People are after money. People fight for money. People sweat for money. People cheat for money. People do anything and everything to have money.

In my opinion, here there is a lack of proper education or lack of understanding or lack of awareness or lack of the universal concepts…

In fact, money and happiness are abundantly available in the universe. There can be millions of millionaires. Everyone can be happy. The whole world can be peaceful, everyone can be rich, and everyone can be happy.

Happiness is everyone's birthright. Only a few claim it.

Abundance is everyone's birthright. Only a few claim it.

Peace is everyone's birthright. Only a few claim it.

Love is everyone's birthright. Only a few claim it.

Success is everyone's birthright. Only a few claim it.

My analogy is like this:

Everyone is born with different genes. Everyone has taken birth in different families with different backgrounds. Everyone has different physical, mental and intellectual capabilities. Everyone has different exposures. Everyone has different friends with different natures. Everyone had different education. Everyone has different resources. Everyone has different connections. Everyone has different approach.

This background, connections, exposure, education and intellectual capabilities are different for every individual and hence everyone is unique in their own way. Everyone is good in some or other field. These all factors lead to different directions, different levels of standards and different lives and lifestyles.

Everyone is unique. Everyone has different destinations. We cannot compare two different people and criticize them for their different states. Life is like a chess game. Different moves lead to different positions and different results. The permutations and combinations of life are infinite. Life is beyond prediction most of the time.

However, for a person who is determined, destined, and focused, none of these factors matter.

We have innumerable examples in history. There are many successful people who were born in poor families. They are many rich people who were born in slums. They are many people in high positions even if they are from ordinary families with minimum back ground.

We have seen people from zero to a hero, people from rags to riches. People from a small village of a country became the leader of the country. People with no money became millionaires or even billionaires. People with no education became biggest entrepreneurs. Everything and anything is possible. History is the proof.

I always admire Sachin Tendulkar. He is from an ordinary middle-class family. But he found his passion, which is cricket. He went after his passion and mastered it and proved to the world. Then money, name, fame and everything started coming to him. He was never after money. He was after his passion.

Roger Federer was another great example. He is from a middle-class family. He found his passion, which is tennis. He went after his passion. Then money, name and fame started coming to him. He was not after money. He was after his passion.

Michael Jackson is another example. He is from an ordinary family. He found his passion, which is singing and dancing. He went after his passion. Then money, name and fame started coming to him. He was not after money. He was after his passion.

Barrack Obama is from a middle-class family. He became the President of the United States.

Abdul Kalam is from a poor family in India. Later he became one of the biggest scientists and also the President of India.

Nelson Mandela is from a poor family. He became the President of South Africa.

Bill Gates was a dropout from college. He has become a billionaire with his entrepreneurial skills.

Steve Jobs is from an ordinary family. He became the Billionaire from Apple.

Narendra Modi was a tea boy at an early age. He became the Prime Minister of India.

There are innumerable numbers of examples in the history to prove that nothing is impossible. Life can turn to different directions. Life can change 180 degrees. Life can evolve in to any shape or size or state.

Find your passion, master it and prove it to the world, and then the world will give you everything. This is a simple success formula.

Also, I observed those who keep up their commitments derive more joy and happiness in their lives. Most importantly keep up your commitments to yourself. That improves confidence and self-esteem which leads to more happiness.

When you want to wake up at a certain time, you should try to keep up your commitment. Every small win will lead to happiness and success. Small acts done consistently lead to bigger results. Consistency is the key.

Abundance mentality also brings more happiness. Scarce mentality will bring sorrow. Always feel abundant. There is abundance everywhere. Happiness is abundantly available free of cost, but people prefer to choose sorrow. I don't understand why?

Gratitude brings happiness. Always be thankful for what you have rather than complaining about what you don't have. That attitude of gratitude attracts more blessings and happiness in life. When you are thankful, the universe reciprocates with more blessings.

Compliment, not complain. By complimenting others, we feel happy. By complaining to others, we make two souls unhappy: ours and others. Complimenting is a habit or attitude that can be learnt. Even complaining is a habit that can be unlearned.

Helping others selflessly brings more happiness. Always be service-oriented every minute and every day of life. That gives immense joy, satisfaction, happiness and a feeling of true accomplishment.

Look at nature and appreciate the beauty and the creation of God. When you embrace the beauty of nature, you are embracing the feeling of joy. That's why people go on holidays to the beaches, mountaintops, or forests, or valleys, or waterfalls. Nature has magnetism. Nature has a stress-absorbing nature. Nature has the pleasant quality of spreading joy, peace and happiness. Nature is like a shock absorber. If you walk by the creek or woods or lake, you can feel the pleasantness, peace and serenity. That's why vacations rejuvenate people.

Even water has stress absorbing nature. When you put your feet in the water, you feel good. When you swim you feel good. When you take bath, you feel good. Water is a powerful stress absorber.

Perfume is also a stress absorber. When you spray lavender or sandalwood or rose perfume in your room or house, you will feel the pleasantness. That's why in a spa, they keep aromatic fragrances to create that pleasant atmosphere to bring joyful feelings and moments.

Good ideas and creative ideas bring happiness. If you want to get an idea, walk for a while. If you want an idea, pause for a while. If you want an idea, look for a while. If you want an idea, close your eyes for a while. If you want an idea, look up for a while. If you want an idea, wash your face for a while. If you want an idea, sip coffee for a while. These few seconds or moments of ritual will change your mood and result in creative ideas. **Moments make moods, and moods make a man.**

When we feel good, energy flows. When we don't feel good, energy blocks. That's why it's very important that we should always try to feel good. Feel good not only for ourselves but also for others. When we feel good about others, energy flows, and it makes a connection. When we don't feel good about others, it creates a disconnection.

Flash Thought:

Somewhere, I read that we can't give others what we don't have. We can give others only what we have. If we have love, we give love. If we have hatred, we give hatred. If we have anger, we give anger. If we have compassion, we show compassion. If we are happy, we can give happiness. If we are sad, we spread sadness. If we have money, we can give money. If we have food, we can give food. If we have knowledge, we can give knowledge. If we have an abundance mentality, we give abundance. If we have a scarcity mentality, we show a scarcity nature.

In a nutshell, we can give what we have. Our attitude, behaviour, manners, character and persona are clear reflections of what we have inside. I strongly believe this.

***

Expectation is the root cause of unhappiness and sorrow in life. We always expect something and if that doesn't happen we become gloomy and we feel we are lost.

As it was mentioned in Bhagavat Geetha, we should

put all our efforts and do our best. But then leave the result to God. He will take care.

But we are always attached to the end result. That brings all unwanted things into our lives.

If we don't get a promotion, we get disappointed.

If our child doesn't come 1st in the class, we get disappointed.

If we don't win a lottery, we get disappointed.

If our boss says something, we get disappointed.

If our car breaks down, we get frustrated.

If we miss the train, we get agitated.

If someone overtakes our car, we get furious.

If we observe the pattern, the root cause of all these feelings is within ourselves. What happens to us is only 10%, but how we react to it decides the balance of 90%.

As we discussed before, we cannot give others what we don t have. We can only give what we have. All these feelings are hidden within us looking for opportunity to come out whenever possible.

We create our feelings. External things are only

triggers. When something happens, we react immediately. That's why Dr Steven Covey clearly mentioned "Be Proactive".

Carry the calmness with you always. Carry the happiness with you always. Carry the patience with you always. Carry cheerfulness always with you. Wherever you are, these are your assets, and they should be with you. Many people think car, house and other things are their assets. But in fact, happiness, cheerfulness, calmness, peace, patience, smile, laughter & light-mindedness are our real assets. If we have these assets, even if we don't have other material assets, life will be peaceful and joyful. We need to realize this. This is true awareness and knowledge.

I read in one of the books a formula called "Intention, Attention & No Tension" (IAN). You can have a good intention. It can be your goal, dream or whatever you want to achieve or become. Then you should pay attention and put all your best efforts to attain that desired goal or dream. And then, you should have no tension at all. You must be open to any outcome that comes after your efforts.

When we are open, then universe surprises us by

giving us more than what we desire. That's the nature of universe. Nature always wants us to be happy.

But our attachment to a particular, specific result causes all wrong things in our life. That means we are not open to accept whatever comes. We are restricting ourselves. We are limiting ourselves. That will limit our achievements too. That will bring down our results too.

When we are open we get far beyond our expectations. When we are close minded, we only get disappointments, frustrations and stress.

Stress is always self-created. No one gives us stress. But we misinterpret things, persons and happenings differently and we feel stressed. Who causes stress? External things are only triggers. Then, the stress comes out from inside of us.

People say my boss is giving me stress, some may say my spouse is giving me stress. Some say my children are giving me stress. But all these people are doing their jobs as per their limited capabilities or capacities. No one is born perfect and everyone cannot be at the same level. They don't have any intention to harm you, but it is their capacity. This is what they can do.

Now we have to accept that everyone has limitations and we cannot change others. Always change starts from within ourselves. If we can change, the whole world can change. MAN changes, GAME changes.

If our rituals are in alignment with the universe and best practices, we always get the best outcomes and best results. This is my conviction.

The more we have gratitude for what we have, the more we get what we want. The more we complain that we don't have, the more we don't get what we want, and also, we may lose what we have. This is a universal phenomenon.

Always be thankful. Always be grateful. Always be cheerful. Always be helpful. Always keep smiling. Always keep serving. Always compliment the good things. Always appreciate God and the Universe for what we have. Always say prayers for the mercy of God upon you. Always pray for the welfare and betterment of others. Always think good of others. Always keep doing small, kind acts to others without expecting anything. Always spread laughter and joy around you. Always make your home a heavenly abode. Always think good of your neighbour. Always spread love to all the people around you. Always try to be kind to whoever crosses your path.

Always be in prayerful attitude. Always be open to accept whatever life is going to throw at you. Always have balance. Always be proactive. Always be a protagonist. Always be positive. Always be optimistic. Always be energetic. Always be healthy. Always have an abundant mentality. Always be a giver. Always be a positive thinker. Always be expecting more good things in life. Always pray for peace and happiness for everyone around you, for the whole society and for the whole world. Always keep affirming positive words. Always speak kind words. Always be nice to people. Always spread positivity around you.

Always keep motivating. Always keep inspiring. Always keep sharing. Always keep caring. Always keep manifesting good things for you and for everyone around you. Always show your happiness in everything you do. Always be passionate. Always be a dreamer. Always keep aiming high. Always try to be your best. Always keep striving. Always keep thriving. Always put your best efforts. Always give all you can.

Always remember sky is the limit. Always think you are unstoppable. Always think that nothing can stop you. Always think that the universe is with you to make your dreams come true. Always feel that whatever is happening in your life is for your own good. Always learn lessons from everything. Always see things with an optimistic eye. Always extend your hands to serve others. Always be happy!!

The world is a huge library. We can read nature, we can read places, we can read people and we can learn a lot from everyday happenings in our life.

In fact, we can learn from every incident happening in our life. We must be observers at every point. When we have observing and learning attitude, life teaches us lessons every minute, every hour, every day of our life.

Our life is nothing but an evolvement of our learning's. Everyone has different perspectives on different things. But observation and learning's can change our perspectives and can bring a paradigm shift in our life. Please be an observant and be in a learning mode.

When I was a child, I heard a story about a frog in a well. The frog used to think that the well is the whole world. One day, rain came, and the water level in the well increased, and finally, the frog came out of the well. Then she saw that the world was much bigger. That's a paradigm shift to that frog. Same way, when we see the world and explore the happenings around us, we get different perspectives.

Those who travel a lot and have seen different countries can understand different cultures & the variety and differences in different parts of the world. But when you are not exposed to the outer world, our thinking cannot be bigger and our understanding cannot be wider.

Travel more, explore more and become wiser.

If we get what we want,
that's a blessing. If we
don't get what we want,
that's destiny. If we get
what we don't want, that's
life.
Blessed Morning !!

PASSION PRASAD

Chapter 7

What Everyone Wants To Achieve

Everyone on earth wants to be happy…

Everyone on earth wants to be rich….

Everyone on earth wants to be beautiful and handsome…

Everyone on earth wants to be famous….

Everyone on earth wants to be loved…

Everyone on earth wants to be appreciated…

Everyone on earth wants to be acknowledged…

Everyone on earth wants to be accepted….

And many more….

There are billions of people on this planet.

But,

Why are all not happy?

Why are all not rich?

Why are all not famous?

Why are all not appreciated?

Why are all not acknowledged?

Well, there can be several reasons. Let us try to list down some of the reasons…

1.   They don't have money…

2.   Their family is from a different background

3.   They are not educated…

4.   They live in a small town…

5.   They don't have sufficient facilities.

6.   They don't have proper infrastructure.

7.   They have some personal challenges…

8.   They are not exposed to the wider society…

9.   They don't have the right connections…

And many more reasons….

Why this dissimilarity or differences or deprivations in society?

We cannot debate on this subject. It depends on many factors that are beyond our control, understanding, and approach.

The country may be underdeveloped or economically challenged. The government structure can be different.

The politicians may be corrupt.

The facilities are not adequate.

Not enough schools.

Education may be costly.

Cost of living is high.

The family doesn't have a sound financial background.

People may have limited physical, mental, or intellectual abilities.

People are not exposed to the modern world.

Technology is not within their reach.

Poor transport facilities.

Disputes/Differences in the family

The justice system is not appropriate.

Like this we can list innumerable number of reasons for the differences in individual's role / capacity in the society.

When you are happy internally, you will be happy externally. Our outer world is just a reflection of our inner world. As I mentioned many times before, we are the creators of our destiny with our thoughts.

We can manifest anything we want just by altering thoughts and mindset.

Flash Thought :

Today is Sunday. I woke up late. My alarm is ringing indicating that this is Book Writing Time. Immediately, I rushed to the washroom and got ready. As usual, I need to take my dogs for a walk. I did and came back to my workstation to commence my book writing. This is what My Mentor, Dr Kailash, said, "Consistency is the Key and the King". Whether you feel like it or not, whether you are on time or not, whether you wake up early or late, continue what you are supposed to do. This is the best practice that gives the best results in due course of time.

***

Flash Thought :

I must confess that every night, I sleep with 3 Angels. One is my beloved wife, and the other 2 are our darling dogs, Skylar & Milar. Skylar is the Mother and is 14 years old, still hale and healthy.

Milar, 4 years old, is her daughter. Skylar has a son also of 4 years, "Marvel", staying in Dubai with one of our friends. I would just like to express my gratitude and thankfulness to the universe for all the blessings in my life. Truly, I am Blessed.

***

Flash Thought:

When the number of hospitals increase, patients will increase…

When the colleges increase, students will increase…

When the protection increases, crime increases…

When the subsidies increase, corruption increases….

When the books increase, readers increase…..

***

Flash Thought:

I want to emphasize the power of "pause" and the power of saying "No". Life is not what happens to us, but how we react to it. Whenever something happens to us in life, just give a pause. This gives us time to reflect on the situation and circumstances. It gives us emotional space to grasp the clear picture and to find clarity of the scenario. Then try to use your wisdom to respond wisely and calmly and coolly.

As Dr Steven Covey says, there is a gap between the stimulus and our response. That gap decides our wisdom and decides our destiny. If something is in the direction of our passion or dream or our goals, we can say "Yes" confidently and joyfully. But if something is against our principles and path, saying "No" is nothing wrong. It emphasizes our dignity and self-esteem.

***

We cannot have the same energy every day. Some days we wake up with high energy and some days we will be with low energy. But discipline can bring balance in our energies. Strong, regular and consistent rituals can make our everyday the same.

Mohammed Ali once said that he hates to wake up every day early in the morning to do his regular practice. But even if he did not like to do so, he had the discipline to do it every day consistently. That's why he became the World Champion in Boxing. We are all the same, but our disciplines are different, and that's why we are different and our destinies are different. Those who have discipline their destiny will be different because their decisions will be different.

As someone said, we are the product of our choices and decisions. Life is a series of choices and decisions. Which school to go to, which course to take up, which country to go to, whom to marry, which job to take up, which car to buy, which house to acquire, where shall we send our children to study etc. In a day, we face hundreds of choices, and we make hundreds of decisions. In the end, our life is the net result of choices and decisions we make. If we track our decisions, we can predict our destiny.

This process is same for every individual wherever he is. We have to face every day. Everyday throws challenges. Every day shows choices. Everyday offers opportunities to take decisions. Those challenges, choices and decisions lead to net results. This is common for everyone on this planet.

***

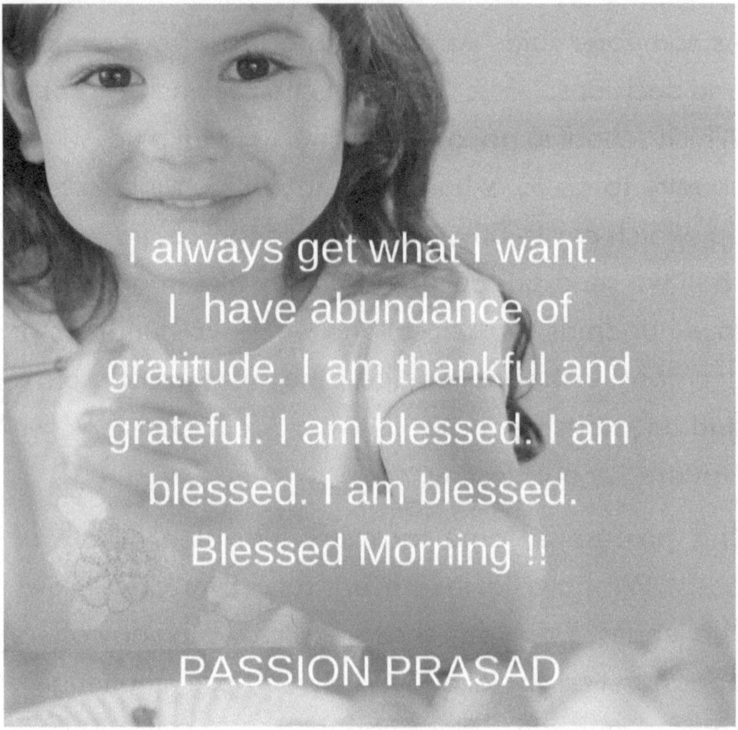

I always get what I want.
I have abundance of
gratitude. I am thankful and
grateful. I am blessed. I am
blessed. I am blessed.
Blessed Morning !!

PASSION PRASAD

Chapter 8

Goals

Everyone wants to achieve something. Every soul on this earth aspires to achieve something, to become something. Some know it as crystal clear and some are not aware of it. Whatever it is, this is defined as goal.

Goals are different from person to person. The means to achieve the goals are different from person to person. Two people may have same goals, but their approaches can be completely different. We cannot compare or condemn the goals of others as it is their life and their dreams and their goals. Human beings are absolutely free to choose their dreams and goals in their life. There are no rules or regulations to impose on people's goals and dreams.

Flash Thought:

We have a practice to say prayers with few neighbours once every week. When we say prayers we feel happy. Prayers bring peace. Prayers protect like a shield.

***

Nothing can be done overnight. Everything has a process. Little by little, brick by brick, day by day, huge monuments can be built and even mega goals can be achieved. This is not a rocket science, but a systematic process.

Burj Khalifa, the Great Wall of China, the biggest bridges, the tallest buildings and many huge projects are the goals of some individuals or groups of people. But they collectively put efforts into making their dreams come true.

Everyone can reach their goal. No one can say I cannot do this. History has innumerable examples. People can do wonders with their determination, focus, hard work, will power and passion.

Sportsmen set new records and beat past records. How is it possible? Because they believe they can do it. They don't believe in limitations. The sky is the only limit, and there is no sky. That means there is no limit to anything.

Can you believe challenged people running marathons, swimming and doing all things that even fully fit persons were not able to do? It's the power of that individual, his determination and desire to get things done. Passion gets results, but passion needs perseverance and perspiration.

People used to travel in ships centuries back. But now there are airplanes to reach any country or continent with ease. People used to send letters by post which used to take days or months to reach. But now with the help of internet we can send messages within no time. People used to make calls by telephone. But now mobiles made things very easy, comfortable and affordable.

History has infinite examples of miracles. These all were goals earlier. But the goals have been achieved. Nothing is impossible. One just needs focus and zeal to get things done.

I live in UAE. I really salute the Rulers of this country. They have a vision. They want to be the first in many things in the whole world and they could achieve it. This is a peaceful country with low crime rate and there is full safety and security to the residents. I truly admire the Visionary Leaders of this country. I am happy and proud to be living in this country at the moment.

<u>Flash Thought:</u>

Just go there to get inspired. You can create a corner or place or a quote or a scenery or a portrait by looking at which you get inspired. Like you see "Smoking zone" or "Children's Area" in malls or parks, you have to create a special place for you by going where you can switch your mood and mindset. I tried this and it worked wonders for me. Whenever I go for morning walk and be amid nature, I get inspired.

I have a portrait of a beautiful quote in my house. Whenever I go there, I feel like pumping my fist. It gives me inspiration. It makes me motivated. Even if I am in the wrong mood, when I go to that place, I become normal, excited and energized. This can be called "Mood Switch Zone", "Motivation Corner", or "My Delight Place". You can name whatever you like. The summary is it keeps your energies high. Try it - you will like it.

***

All the biggest companies in the world and biggest brands in the world have their base in the UAE. UAE is an attraction for travellers from all around the world.

The biggest malls and other attractions are available here. These were all goals of the Rulers, and today, they have become a reality. They are building the biggest airport in the world. They have Burj Al Arab, the only 7-star hotel in the world. Atlantis Hotel and the Aquarium are all wonders. But they were dreams and goals earlier. Today, they became a reality.

This all proves and shows that nothing is impossible. You just need to work relentlessly towards your dream. You need strong support of qualified people in different fields to achieve your goals and dreams. There you need the help of a mentor.

This reminds me that Roger Federer is a giant in Tennis. But he had a coach. Is the coach a better player than him? Maybe or maybe not. However, the guidance of a coach or mentor brings discipline and system to our practice and will help us achieve our goals. Tiger Woods was a great golf player, but he, too, had a coach. Everyone needs a mentor to bring discipline and to direct all our efforts, focus and energy in the right direction to achieve our dreams or goals. Have a mentor in life. It can be anyone. It can be your father, mother, brother, sister or a friend or any other external person. However, having a mentor will help one to speed up the process of achieving his or her goals.

Everyone has strengths and weaknesses. Wise men find their weaknesses and try to overcome them and in turn convert them in to their strengths.

<u>Flash Thought :</u>

My father told me a story.

Someone asked a learned person, "Why the President or the King of a country has big huge palaces and hundreds of servants, assistants, gardeners, secretaries and so many cars? Is this not a national wastage of money?

One learned person answered this way. He asked "What a normal person or citizen thinks in his life? Everyone will be thinking about making money to feed his family, making money to send his children to school, making money to pay the rents and bills, to build a house, to get their children married and to provide some safety and security to his family. Normal personal always thinks this way. Will you agree?

If the president or the king has to think about making money for his children, for the bills, and for the family, then how can he think about the country or a nation? When the mind is occupied with thoughts for the safety and security of the family, one cannot think or focus on the whole country. When there is an assurance that even if anything happens to him at any time, his family will be taken care of for generations, then only he can focus and think about the nation. When we have problems in the house, we don't even think about our neighbours.

So, when there is assurance, guarantee, safety, security and confirmation that even if I die this moment, my family is safe and will be well taken care of, then only I can think of other people and the country.

That's why there are people, servants, secretaries at every step for his assistance, rescue and to give him peace of mind about his family so that he can solely and entirely and absolutely focus on the country and its welfare.

This logic is well-settled in my mind. This is true, isn't it?

If we have bills to pay and the deadline is coming, we don't care anything else.......

***

Competence brings confidence.
Preparation brings confidence.
Will power brings confidence.
Determination brings
confidence.
Passion brings confidence.
Big dreams bring confidence.
Confident Morning !!

● ● PASSION PRASAD

Chapter 9

Role Of Money In Life

Everyone agrees that money plays a major role in life. Money gives security, money gives peace of mind and money gives joys in life. But money cannot buy happiness.

Some people say that money is the root cause of all evil. But in my opinion, that is a negative approach towards the concept of money. Everyone should make money. Everyone has to live their life. We need to pay the bills, pay the rent, buy a house, buy a car, buy gas, need to eat, need to wear clothes. For everything, we need money. We cannot barter goods for getting things in this modern era.

Everyone should make money and then should use some of that money for helping other people in need, for charity purposes and for contributing to the betterment of the world.

People who do not have money know the importance and value of money. People who do not have good health know the importance and value of good health.

People who do not have proper relationships know the importance and value of relationships. People who are not happy know the importance and value of happiness. This analogy proves to me that the lack of something brings awareness of its importance.

Flash Thought:

Few years' back I wrote a quote: "I am not as good as I think, but I am not as bad as you think". In general, we always think high of ourselves and we think low of others in general. But we are in the middle, not that good or not that bad.

We should have self-esteem, but over confidence is always bad. We always find faults with others more than the reality. We try to be extreme rather than to be a moderate. Always balance is the best.

***

Flash Thought:

Whenever we see a person, we immediately create an impression about that person unknowingly based on his appearance or looks or dressing or style of walking or the energy he portrays. This is an instant reaction. But when he starts opening his mouth, says a few words, and starts communicating with us, our impression either changes or gets more confirmed.

Face is the index of the man. Every person has an Aura. We radiate signals. We create an energy halo around us all the time. Whenever we reach within the energy circle of another person our energy gets influenced, our moods get affected and our thoughts get altered.

We always hear "Love at first sight". This is not just because of physical beauty or facial beauty, but the influence of their energy circle. We all have energy. We are like a battery. If we don't charge our battery we get discharged. Charging is in our mind, heart, soul and body.

Be energized and you will be a magnet. When you are looking for love, or for a job or for a friend, it all depends on your energy circle or centre.

***

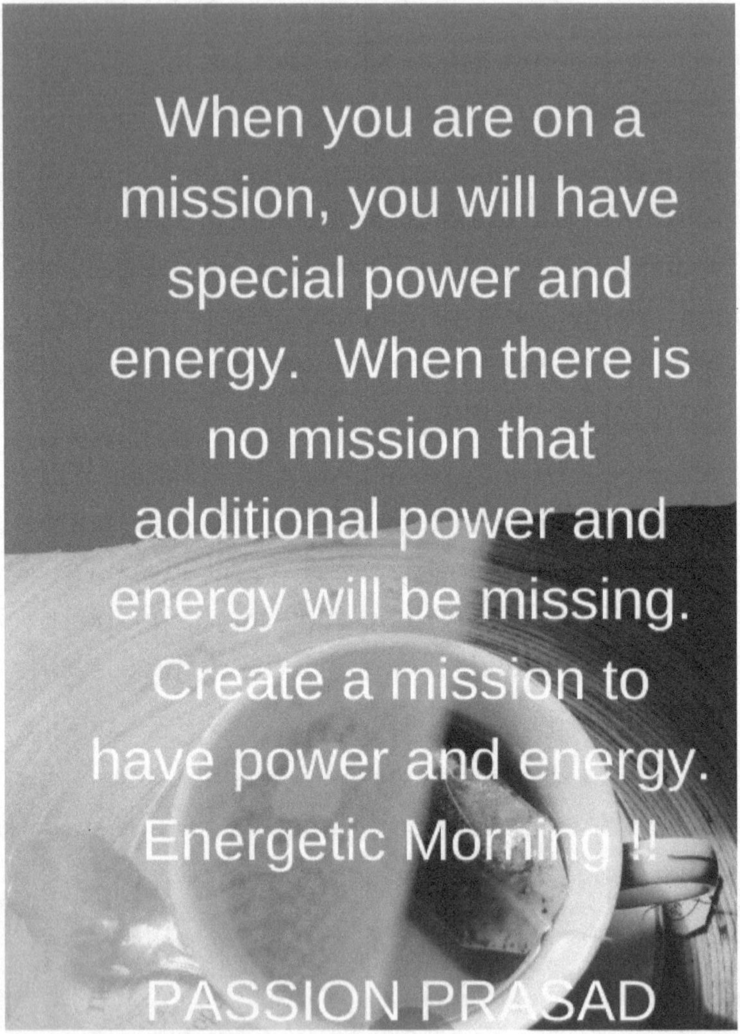

When you are on a mission, you will have special power and energy. When there is no mission that additional power and energy will be missing. Create a mission to have power and energy. Energetic Morning !!

PASSION PRASAD

Chapter 10

Energy Is Everything

Health is wealth. Good health is real wealth. If we have good health we will have energy to do anything or everything. Ultimately energy is everything in real life and in the scientific world and in sport's world and everywhere. If there is no energy, there is no life.

Some people have a lot of money, but no good health. That means there is lack of energy. Some people have not so good relationships. That means there is a lack of energy. Some people don't know what to do. That means there is a lack of energy. Whenever there is no proper alignment, there is lack of energy. When there is energy everything falls in place.

Life is like a driving journey. When we drive, there will be some speed breakers. We just need to slow down and pass the speed breakers. Even life is like that, there will be challenges every time. We just need to slow down and face the challenges boldly and cross over them successfully, peacefully and energetically.

When there are speed breakers on the road, we cannot drive at full speed, as it can damage the car or may lead to an accident. It's always wise to slow down and cross the speed breaker with patience. Even facing the challenges of life is the same way. Aggressiveness or impatience will aggravate the situation. It's always wise to cool down and solve the problems of life intelligently, patiently and coolly. Even this is energy management.

Similarly, when we are driving, it's not always a straight line. There will be left turn or right turn, curves, bridges and valleys. Same way, even life is not a straight path. There will be twists and turns, ups and downs, challenges and opportunities. Life is a mixture of all, A to Z. Life is a bundle of everything. Life is not only full of happiness, and life is not only full of challenges. Life is a formula that consists of all derivatives, components, additions, subtractions, multipliers, divisions, and many more. Make use of energy in the right way.

When we are about to drive, it always starts smooth and simple. After some time, we catch up on the highway and can go at full speed. But after some time, narrow lines come, and the traffic increases, and many traffic lights, speed breakers, and many other passengers cross the pedestrian lanes. Even in life, we face similar situations. Sometimes, life goes very smoothly, but suddenly, something happens, and life turns 180 degrees. Many unexpected things happen, and some unpleasant things may happen. Energy dissipation varied from time to time.

Always this driving journey on a road analogy gives me many solutions and teaches a lot of lessons. If we can behave the same way we drive to the destination with patience, even in life, we can reach the destinations with comfort and ease. This reminds me of Dr Steven Covey's principle, "Begin with the end in mind". Always, we should keep the end in mind. Small challenges and obstacles are part of the journey and part of life. They should not be the main things in our lives.

I always feel a good driver will have a good life, as he knows how to drive. Similarly, a bad driver will have similar life, as he is a bad driver. Driving approach and living life looks me same.

Here, I would like to propose one more approach. Normally, we drive to the office or to any place on the same route always, right? Here, I suggest trying a different route sometimes. This can change your whole experience and energy completely in a new way. If there is the same routine in life, then, at times, life becomes monotonous, and we feel bored. We need variety and spice and change in life to bring back vigour, vitality, charm, enthusiasm and energy. Try different routes and enjoy different experiences.

Another important thing to accept in our lives is that we cannot please everyone on the journey of our lives. Definitely, someone or the other will be unhappy and not pleased with us. It's perfectly ok. We cannot please everyone, and this is the absolute truth of life. People are of different kinds, with different attitudes and varied characters. If someone tries to please everyone, then he or she is not living their authentic life. They just want to please each other by adjusting themselves every time and every second to match each other's opinions and interests. That's not real life.

Another eternal thing I have learned is that no one is eternal. However rich, smart, intelligent, famous, strong, powerful and influential one is, everyone has to age. Ageing is not in our control. No one can control ageing. Cosmetics and other medical drugs can prevent signs of some ageing, but underlying ageing will continue. Everyone's life has to come to an end, however great they are. We have to accept this eternal truth of life and live life the same way. Billions and millions of people came before us on this earth and left. The same story repeats. We come here for a short while, and we have to do our job and leave. Life is like a drama. We are all actors with different characters. We just need to do our part. But whatever we do, we have to try to do our best to leave the best impression on the audience. That's leaving a legacy. Only a few can do that; others do their part without impact and finish it without effectiveness.

Another suggestion I want to emphasize to the readers to keep high energy levels is not to watch the 24-hour news channels too much. They can ruin our thoughts, our feelings, our energy and even our life. These TV channels want to promote their ratings and want to show the prime news of a murder or rape or robbery, or a scandal repeatedly, continuously, several and multiple times every day. This will have a tremendous negative influence and impact on our minds, hearts, health, attitudes, energy and everything else. One should avoid watching these channels as much as possible. If you want to watch the news, just watch for 5 to 10 minutes and stop. But never watch continuously for hours. That can affect your family life, career and everything.

Life is too short to be unhappy. Life is too short to be sad. Life is to enjoy. Life is to serve. Life is to feel abundance. Life is to give. Life is to help others. Life is to be of some help to our neighbours, society, community and wherever and whenever possible. Life is to feel the joys the Almighty has given us and created around us and to enjoy the sunrise and sunset and nature's every season and variation to the utmost. Life is to live with full energy.

Flash Thought:

I started writing my book ten days back. I was writing at least a few pages every day. Suddenly, 2 days back, I fell sick and was admitted to hospital. The doctor said I was dehydrated. I was really feeling very weak. They gave me drips, and I was there for 24 hours.

During that time on the hospital bed, I came to a realization that health is utmost important than anything. I got the opportunity to reflect on myself and why I should take care of my health.

They say, when we are young, we put all efforts to earn money sidelining our health. When we become old we spend all the money to regain our health. Very strange, isn't it? Everyone is aware of this absolute truth, but still, we do the same thing. I guess there should be some lessons in the text books on how to take care of our health and the importance of it...

***

Flash Thought:

Do you know what I do between the four walls of my house? Neither do I know what you do between the four walls of your house. Everyone's life is private. Everyone can live as they like in their private zone or area or place or house. But that is their preparation ground. Once they step out of that place, they have to perform. Here, performance reflects in their communication, in their attitude, in their behaviour, in their character, and in everything they do.

The place we stay is our preparation field, and everything outside of that is the performance field.

***

<u>Flash Thought:</u>

Planning is the biggest key factor in one's success. If planning is proper, process will be smoother and the end result will be greater. But if the planning is poor, process will be complex and end result will be a chaos. Planning has major place in each and everything we do.

I heard that in Japan everything happens exactly on time. Trains arrive exactly at the stipulated time and leave exactly at the right time without even a minute delay. This is example of perfect planning. Of course, mechanization and automatization helps to follow those timings. But definitely sufficient planning is involved in this design and development.

When we want to construct a building, we first need to make the blueprint. Then we try to arrange the raw material, digging, drilling and building everything as per the blueprint. Even in life, if we want to be successful, we need a blueprint of our life. Without a blueprint, life will go without proper direction.

Flash Thought:

The secret of happiness is to have something exciting always to look forward to. If you are planning to go for a vacation, it's something excited to look forward to. If you are getting married it's something you are excited to look forward to. If you are about to get graduated, it's something to look forward to. If you are participating in some sports, it's something to look forward to.

When you have something in the pipeline that is coming up, your energy levels are different. If you are going to your best friend, you will feel a different energy. If you are going on a date with your spouse or loved ones, that is something exciting, too.

Always have something exciting to come up. That will keep your energy levels up.

There is no satisfaction
without sacrifice. Sacrifice can
be money, time, effort, help,
kindness or even a smile.
Without giving away
something, there can't be
satisfaction.
Sacrificing Morning !!

PASSION PRASAD

Chapter 11

How To Contribute To The World

Someone nicely said, "Service is the rent we pay for occupying this earth". In fact, it is everyone's duty to contribute to the betterment of their fellow men, society, community, country, and the world. If we do not contribute or do service to humanity, our mission on this earth is incomplete and ineffective.

God doesn't give everything to one person for long. He holds something in his hands and plays his trump card at vital stages. God is a Master Player. It's our duty to please Him with our good deeds for His blessings and His mercy.

If He gives lot of wealth to one person, he may give challenged relationships or challenged children. If he doesn't give wealth he may give a wonderful partner and beautiful kids. If one spouse is beautiful, the other may not be so. If not wealth, he may give support in his higher education. Something or other will be missing soon from our life, other things being intact.

Service to humanity and Prayers to God will prevent obstacles in our path. For a smooth journey of our life, we need to surrender ourselves to God. Our wealth, our gifts, our talents, our achievements are just mercy of God. We should never forget that. With the click of one button, he can alter our life. He is the omniscient and omnipotent.

When we surrender, we get the best things in life. Just for example, when we go to a doctor, we surrender our body to him for better things to happen. When we go to a barber, we surrender our head to get the best haircut done. When we go for massage, we surrender our body to the masseur to get the best effect. By surrendering we get best service. This is true when we are dealing with the Almighty God.

We can contribute or do service in several ways. It's not always the money. We can offer our time, energy, suggestion, helping hand, empathy, compassion, a hug, a hearing ear and many more.

We can help a person in need.

We can help a child in his education.

We can give a ride to a person in need.

We can give advice to a person in need.

We can offer some financial contribution to charity.

We can donate our eyes when we die.

We can offer consultation to the person in need.

We can give a hearing ear to the person in sorrow.

The list goes on and on…..

But we must serve in different ways. Service should become part of our life, our culture, our attitude, our character, our nature, our spirit, our DNA. No service, no life. It's as simple as that.

Millions of people came here before us. They did some good things, and that's why we are able to live in better conditions today. If we can contribute something good, the coming generations can live in much better conditions here. That should be everyone's wish while doing service.

I like the quote, "You come with nothing and fight for everything, and in the end, you leave everything and go with nothing". What a profound meaning it conveys. Everyone on this earth comes empty-handed and leaves empty-handed. The entire struggle in between is not just for survival but to have as much more as possible. Having more is not bad at all as long as he shares it with the underprivileged and the needy. Whatever is in excess can be contributed to the world.

I like another quote stating that on every tomb there will be year of birth and year of death and a dash in between. What does the dash denote? It defines the life we lived in between our birth and death. If we can make that dash meaningful and impactful, then our life was worth living. If we live for others we do justice to our existence on this earth. If we live for ourselves then we are a burden on this earth.

Flash Thought:

Recently there was a wedding at Ambani's house. I heard that more than three hundred millions of dollars has been spent on this wedding. This is for what? I am not competent enough to comment on someone else's personal life. But this money could have been used more efficiently, more effectively, more graciously and more generously on different projects for the welfare of mankind instead of spending for just family affair. This is my personal opinion. If I am wrong, please ignore this topic.

***

I - Innovations

D - Dreams

E- Experiments

A- Aspirations

S- Simulations

IDEAS is a combination of

all these creative things.

Idea Morning !!

PASSION PRASAD

Chapter 12

All You Need Is One Idea

All we need is one idea. Just one idea! To change our life, to transform our life, to be successful, to be healthy, to be rich, to be productive and to be excellent - what we need is just one idea. There may be hundreds and thousands of ideas in the world or universe. But what we need to implement is just one idea.

When we read any book, we don't remember all the points, suggestions, recommendations, techniques, or lessons from that book. But if we can take home one idea and implement it, that's enough for change.

When we watch a movie or a video, if we can take home one idea, that's enough for change.

One medicine can cure the illness. One day can change life. One person can make a difference. One hug can heal a person. One idea can change a life.

Roger Federer – one idea – Excellence in Tennis

Sachin Tendulkar – one idea – Excellence in Cricket

Lionel Messi – one idea – Excellence in Football

Mohammed Ali – one idea – Excellence in Boxing

Bill Gates – one idea – Excellence in Windows Software

Steve Jobs – one idea – Excellence in technology and design

Thomas Alva Edison – one idea – Light Bulb

Wright Brothers – one idea – Flying plane

Newton - one idea – Gravitation Theory

Mahatma Gandhi – one idea – use of nonviolence

There are billions of examples. All you need is just one idea that can change the trajectory of life by 180 degrees.

How does that idea come? That is the million-dollar question.

Some people have some special skills or interests right from the childhood. If they are serious about it and they can pursue their skills, it can become their passion and their profession and can take them to greater heights in their life.

There are many methods to ignite that idea. Keep learning every day. Keep reading books. When you are turning the pages of some book, suddenly a sentence or a paragraph can attract your attention which resonates with your internal fire. There comes the spark. That's it. The fire is on.

While watching a video, while looking at some advertisements, while looking at some billboards, while talking to someone, while listening to someone, while walking on the street, even while in washroom, while tuning to a song, while traveling, while looking at the sky, while rushing through the hectic day suddenly the sparkling idea can come. That's it. The fire is on.

That "Aha" moment or that "Eureka" moment, or you can call it "your moment", can come at any time. Even while sleeping, the idea can trigger, and suddenly, you may wake up in the middle of the night. That is the game changer. That game-changing moment can come at any moment. And the fire is on.

The most important thing is you should keep looking for that spark that can ignite the fire within you. You should have the zeal within you. You must be hungry. You must be crazy. You must be silly. You must be anything to find that spark. Then the fire is on.

Everyone has some fire within them. We need some external spark that can ignite the fire within us. Some mentors can make that work for you. Some coaches can make that work for you. Some trainers can make it work for you. Some parents can make it work for you. Some friends can make it work for you. Some books can make it work for you. Some videos can make it for you. Some quotes can make it work for you. Some scenery can make it work for you. Some portraits can make it work for you. Keep looking, keep searching, keep exploring, keep adventuring and keep knocking. One fine day, one fine moment, the spark appears....that transforms your entire state. Then the fire is on.

As Tony Robin says, you must be in the peak state to get things done. If your energy does not match, things will not work. If the energy is not there, you cannot see that spark even if it is right in front of your eyes. You will become blind. Vision becomes blurred. You cannot identify things right in front of your eyes. But if you are in the zone, if you are in the right state of mind, if you are ready, if you are with full energy, then the universe will enable you to find that spark. Like Steve Jobs says, "Stay hungry, stay foolish..."

All you need is just one idea.

Rajnikanth is a famous south Indian film star. If you read his life story, it's very interesting. He was a bus conductor in a southern city. He issued tickets to the passengers in a bus. But somehow one day the spark came and his life changed 180 degrees. I highly recommend you to read his story. Now he is a superstar of India and for him sky is the only limit.

The spark can come in different shades, different shapes, different suites and different ways. It can be through a person or through a product, or through an action or through a sentence or through a word or through a silence. Just keep looking. Stay Hungry, Stay Foolish….

A newspaper seller got that spark and became a billionaire.

A street vendor found his spark and became a celebrity.

A housewife found her spark and became the biggest author.

A child found her spark and became a successful singer.

A shoe polisher found the spark and became a big entrepreneur.

A tea boy found the spark and became the Prime Minister of the country.

Keep looking. Stay hungry....

Most beautiful things come out of ugly sources. Most powerful things come out of powerless things. The origin and destination will not have any connection at all. It's a mystery.

The parents may not be beautiful, but the daughter may become Miss World. The parents may not be rich, but the son may become a billionaire. The parents may not be healthy, but their son can become the biggest wrestler. The background and the future end may never match at all.

I always admire Imran Khan of Pakistan. He was a great cricket player of international fame. I understand he is from a very ordinary family. But he has charisma and a persona that has attracted many people. Even Princess Diana got attracted to him and visited Pakistan to meet him. Later Imran Khan became the Prime Minister of Pakistan. I truly admire him. His origin and destination are far too different.

But he found his spark....

I would like to repeat the story of Narendra Modi once again. He was a tea boy in a tiny restaurant in a small corner of a small town in a state of India. He became the Prime Minister of India. That is the spark I am talking about. From where to where...

Origin and destination have no connection at all...

I always admire Arnold Schwarzenegger. He came from a small country to the USA maybe with a pair of clothes. But he found his spark. He found his passion in bodybuilding. Later, he became the world champion, not once but 6 times, I guess. He became a highly-paid Hollywood star. Later, he became the Governor of California. All I can say is he found his spark...

Let me not miss my hero, Sylvester Stallone. He sold his dog for few bucks to be able to eat. He became the best body builder and very highly paid Hollywood Actor. All I can say is, he found his spark.

You, I, and everyone else can find that spark. It doesn't cost money. Money was never a problem at all. Just keep looking. Stay hungry, stay foolish...

In one of the speeches of Steve Jobs, he mentions

about connecting the dots. Life is nothing but connecting the dots. But we cannot connect the dots forward. When we connect the dots backward, then we can get the whole picture. Find your dots which can weave a beautiful necklace.....

Extraordinary comes from ordinary. No one is born extraordinary. Everyone was born ordinary, but everyone has the potential to become extraordinary. Where does that potential lie? Find the spark, and you will be extraordinary....

Like Jim Kwik, the Memory Coach, says, "Knowledge is not power, but knowledge is potential power".

Many people know what to do, but they don't do it.

Many people know how to do it, but they don't do it.

Dr Steven Covey mentions in his book of "7 Habits of Highly Effective People", there is Skill, Knowledge & Desire to do. The overlapping of these 3 is the habit, most potential zone.

Skill – What to do

Knowledge – How to do

Desire – Want to do

I like Vishen Lakhiani of MindValley. His life story is

very touching and powerful inspiration. Again, his origin and his destination have no connection at all. From humble beginnings he rose to noble callings. From nowhere, he reached everywhere. Amazing guy….

Believe in yourself. All you need is one idea….

I read in one of Brain Tracy's talks, one person came to United States with nothing and in the immigration they found nothing. But later that person became one of the biggest entrepreneurs and a billionaire and gave employment to millions of people. Where was that potential?? Everything is in our minds. All you need is one idea…..

I listened to one of Robin Sharma's speech. He met a janitor in the washroom of an airport. I don't remember the names exactly. But that janitor had a spark in him. Robin Sharma found that spark and he interviewed him. That janitor mentioned that the wash room he cleans is his office. He said whoever enters his office should leave with a smile and pleasant feelings. Wow, what a great concept…

My Friend, Sameer Geepee wrote an article on LinkedIn about one barista in a café in Dubai. That barista had a spark. His smile and his debonair attitude attracted Sameer Geepee and he interviewed him and posted on LinkedIn. I give credit to both of them. One has the spark within him and the other has eyes to be able to detect that spark.

Another friend of mine, Nisha Shivram is a Toastmaster from humble beginnings. She found her spark and she became the 2nd Runner Up in the World Public Speaking Championship. From where to where? All you need is one idea.....

Another friend of mine, Anshu Jain, a great anchor and Emcee for many popular programs on mega stages, from where to where? She found her spark. All you need is one idea....

I would like to mention the name of one more person who was my boss in my earlier company, Mr Rappai. He came to Qatar for a job as an accountant. He is from a simple background and from a small family of a small town in Kerala. Now he is a Billionaire and CEO of a Billion-dollar company in Qatar. From where to where? All you need is one idea....

This reminds me the name of Ralph Smedley, the founder of Toastmasters. He started toastmasters in a garage and later it became international with thousands of toastmaster clubs in the world. From where to where....

Another name is Ivan Misner, the founder of BNI International, from a small corner in United States to all around the world. From nowhere to everywhere. All you need is just one idea....

Tony Robins - From nowhere to everywhere...

Brian Tracy – From nowhere to everywhere....

Jack Canfield – From nowhere to everywhere

Ziz Ziglar – From nowhere to everywhere...

Bob Proctor – From nowhere to everywhere...

Les Brown – From nowhere to everywhere....

Jim Rohn – From nowhere to everywhere...

Robin Sharma – From nowhere to everywhere....

Vishen Lakhiani – From nowhere to everywhere....

All you need is one idea......

I take this opportunity to mention about another friend Mr EP Abulrehiman in Qatar. He started his journey as a sales executive in a pharmaceutical company. Today he is a CEO of a million-dollar company with hundreds of branches in different countries of Middle East. From nowhere to everywhere. All you need is one idea….

There are many great people on this planet. There is plenty of good on this earth. We always focus on what is wrong and what is bad. But, in spite of all the wrong and bad in the world, the world is surviving and thriving because of the goodness and greatness in the world. Let's have more goodness in the world. Let's have more greatness in the world. All you need is one idea….

It reminds me of my friend, Mr Shridhar Sampath, from Dubai. He is a Trainer, Motivational Speaker and Author. He came from humble beginnings but rose to greater heights with his passion. From nowhere to everywhere…

It reminds me of a great person by the name of Mr Gopal Balasubramaniam. He works for KPMG in Qatar. He is an example of "From Zero to Hero". He started his career with a small job. But today, he is a prominent person in the whole of Qatar. He is another example of "From nowhere to everywhere". His passion for narrating stories of all his happenings in life and meetings with prominent people on his

Facebook wall is his trademark. His ever-smiling face is like a beacon for many.

Another great example is my friend, Abdul Nasar from Qatar. His life started with humble beginnings. But he found his spark at one point in his life and his life turned 180 degrees. He has participated in all major Marathons and Triathlons in the world. From nowhere to everywhere. All you need is one idea....

Another friend is Nisar from Pakistan. His passion for solar energy is so powerful that he became one of the Board Members of SEAP (Solar Energy Association of Pakistan). From nowhere to everywhere. All you need is one idea....

Another stalwart is Mr Sony Varghese from Qatar. He came more than 5 decades back to Qatar. Started small, but today he is one of the prominent persons in Qatar and has President's Citation Award from the President of Toastmasters International. From nowhere to everywhere. All you need is one idea....

Another example is Mr Rajeswar Sundareshan. He also started his career as an Accountant in Qatar. Now he is one of the prominent persons in Qatar and is on the Internal Board of Directors of International

Chartered Accounts Association. From nowhere to everywhere. All you need is one idea…

One more person that comes to my mind is my best friend Rammohan Rai. His ever smiling and ever energetic look made him a debonair person. He never gets aged..

Another person who comes to my mind is Mr Bijay Shah. He came from South Africa to United Arab Emirates. He started with humble beginnings. Now he is the National Director of BNI of many countries and is a prominent person in Dubai. From nowhere to everywhere. All you need is one idea….

From nowhere to everywhere do not mean the riches or the fame they have acquired. But the spark that got ignited in them followed by hard work that resulted in their personal and professional success. Money is just a byproduct. Passion is the key. If you are passionate about something and master that art or field and prove your worth, money will pour in to your pocket without even your knowledge. All you need is one idea….

One more example is Mr Ram Ganglani from Dubai. He came here few decades back and started small trainings for individuals and corporates. Later he started inviting big giants like Jack Canfield, Brian Tracy and many others. He has become a successful CEO of a large training company and made a difference in many lives. From nowhere to everywhere. All you need is one idea....

We can learn, emulate and implement many lessons from all these successful stalwarts. Everyone is a book. We can learn a lot of lessons from everyone. The world is a huge library with different books, live streams and natural wonders. Everything is ready to inspire the readers if they are ready. Are you ready?

We can take how much ever we can. It is an ocean. Some take with a cup. Some take with a mug. Some take with a bucket. Some take with a huge container. It all depends on one's individual capacity. But there is plenty for everyone. It never empties, but gets refilled every time....

Everyone has a mind and heart. Every heart can be as big as the ocean. But some people play it small. Every mind is capable of achieving everything infinitely. But some people play it small. Play big and show the world that you are utilizing your mind and heart to the fullest extent. Learn as much as you can with your brain, and give as much as you can with your heart.

Mind is a taker, and Heart is a giver. Try to use both. Take as much you can and give as much as you can. Don't just take, but keep giving.

Knowledge and wisdom are to be shared. The world needs givers in every form. Teachers play a major role. Trainers play a major role. Coaches play a major role. Speakers play a major role. Authors play a major role. They are all givers. Today's reader may become tomorrow's author. Today's taker may become tomorrow's giver. Unless you take, you cannot give. Unless you have it, you can't give it. Have the knowledge to give it back. Have money to give it back. Have the energy to give it back. Have health to give it back. Have everything you can to give it back. AI like the BNI's slogan, "Giver's Gain". The more you give, the more you gain. But to give first, you have to take it in the form of learning, knowledge, lessons, wisdom and education. Then, you will be in a better position to share what you have.

Every day will not be the same. Some days are sunny, some days are cloudy, some days are rainy and some days are windy. But if one has strong rituals, supporting family and self-control, everyday can be a beautiful day.

Everyday morning we should have a robust ritual that can set our mood for the day. Do something, read something, watch something or talk to someone that can ignite the spark in the morning which can propel the engine for the rest of the day.

All you need is one idea for change...

All you need is one idea for transformation...

All you need is one idea for innovation...

All you need is one idea for success...

All you need is one idea to make money...

All you need is one idea to fix relationships...

All you need is one idea to get good health...

All you need is one idea to make a difference...

All you need is one idea to serve mankind...

All you need is one idea for anything worth doing...

When you want an idea, walk for a while. When you want an idea, pause for a while. When you want an idea, look for a while. When you want an idea, close eyes for a while. When you want an idea, look up for a while. When you want an idea, be silent for a while. Ideas Morning!!

PASSION PRASAD

Chapter 13

Power Of Prayer

The power of prayer is infinite, immense and unexplainable. Prayers can do wonders. Prayers can do miracles. Prayers are positive. Prayers are powerful.

Below are a few excerpts of a few religions on Prayers.

Hinduism:

Prayer is considered to be an integral part of the Hindu religion; it is practiced during Hindu worship and is an expression of devotion. The chanting of mantras is the most popular form of worship in Hinduism. The Vedas are liturgical texts (mantras and hymns). Stuti is an umbrella term for religious literary creations, but it literally means "praise."

Christianity:

Prayer is communication with God. We do this by praising Him, confessing our sins before Him, thanking Him and asking Him for our needs and desires. Prayer is communion with our Creator. When we pray, we engage in loving fellowship with the Maker of heaven and earth.

Islam:

In Islam, prayer, supplication, purification and most ritual actions are considered acts of worship (Ibaadat). The most well-known and obligatory act in Islam is the performance of the five daily prayers, which in Arabic is known as salah (often written salat).

Buddhism:

Buddhist prayer, a fundamental spiritual practice within Buddhism, serves as a means to cultivate mindfulness, compassion, and a deep connection with the divine aspects of the universe. Buddhist prayers are often expressions of gratitude, compassion, and the aspiration for enlightenment for all sentient beings.

Baha'i Faith:

In the Baháí writings, the purpose of prayer is to get closer to God and to help better their own conduct and to request divine assistance. Prayer is used to express an individual's love of God and to affect their inner self.

Judaism:

The Torah refers to prayer as "the service of the heart," an act suffused with love and reverence. Prayer is about a child approaching his loving parent. In fact, the medieval sage Maimonides writes that "prayer without concentration is akin to a lifeless body."

***

There are many religions in the world and I do respect each and every religion. If I fail to mention the name of any religion, my sincere apologies, as my knowledge is very limited in this aspect. Readers may please forgive me.

But the essence of prayers from the scriptures of all religions is communion with God, expression of our love to God and to be closer to God. That's why prayers are powerful. The more we pray, the Almighty God will be much more happy and will be send his blessings to us in different forms.

Flash Thought:

No one is happy with what they have. Everyone wants something which they don't have. Everyone tries to find happiness somewhere else. But the truth is happiness is always with us in what we have and how we are. If we can learn the attitude of gratitude and always be thankful for what we have, we can find happiness then and there itself. Happiness is not external somewhere on the mountains or beaches or mansions. Happiness is internal in our tiny minds and cute hearts.

Contentment is in shortage in this competitive world. Everyone tries to chase after something. In this race, most people lose to themselves.

Sincere prayers can bring one to reality and can bring contentment in life.

Prayers give us protection.
Prayers give us confidence.
Prayers give us patience.
Prayers give us peacefulness.
Prayers give us calmness.
Prayers give us Everything.
Prayerful Morning !!

PASSION PRASAD

Chapter 14

Personal Development

All successful people spent time on their personal development. Personal development is not a luxury, it is a necessity. It's an investment for our brighter and better future. If we don't have time for personal development, it's like we don't have time to put gas in our car. Eventually the car stops and eventually the progress of our life stops.

There is no need to stress the importance of personal development in one's life. Everyone should understand to excel in their life or profession or anywhere.

Personal development is the easiest thing these days because of internet and social media. Whatever one wants to learn, they can browse online for the content and can go through the material. We can make our cars an audio universities. We can listen to audios, podcasts and many other things while driving. We can read books. We can watch videos on you tube and other channels. We can attend many courses online or live events.

However, personal development is the easiest part of this era. Previously people have to travel to other places or other countries to get access to these courses or events. Now everything is available at your desk on your computer or our mobile.

There is no excuse if we don't make use of these tools for our personal development. Personal development is in our hands, at our desk, at our place wherever we are. If someone doesn't make use of this, then it is sheer procrastination or lack of awareness or immaturity. Awareness is the liveliest thing in this modern era. We cannot say I am not aware, that means we are not on the right path.

Personal development is of prime importance to everyone. If MAN changes, GAME changes....

Flash Thought:

Beauty is a welcome guest everywhere. Physical beauty will open doors everywhere. But that is not enough to go further. One needs inner beauty, the right attitude, good behaviour and many other things to go to the next level. Physical beauty will help only in the first level of entry. Physical beauty is temporary as it lasts as long as one is at the right age. But once he or she becomes aged, physical beauty vanishes. What lasts forever are inner beauty, kindness, love, compassion and a good attitude.

Flash Thought:

Every country has their own culture, heritage, language, beauty, ethnicity and many more. When you explore different countries, you will witness variety of cultures and will experience beauty of those places. Their history is different, their economy is different, their politics are different, their population is different and their education system is different. Every country is different in its own unique way and nature.

Flash Thought:

Every elderly person has many stories to tell. Elderly people need attention. They need our time. They need our love. They need our care. They want to talk to people. They want to narrate their experiences and their stories and the lessons they have learnt.

Spending quality time with elderly people will help us to enhance our knowledge. Elderly people are like a dictionary. They have ocean of knowledge to share. They have ocean of experience to pour out. Elderly people are assets to cherish.

Flash Thought:

In this modern digital era, mobile is our world. Our whole life is connected with our mobiles and laptops. Laptops are more for content, but mobiles are more for connection, information, exploration, recreation, relaxation and many more.

If we don't have our mobile with us, we may become mad. Our whole life revolves around our mobile. On an average, every person these days looks at his mobile at least every 5 minutes in his day. Even if there are no messages or mails or comments, every person looks at his mobile frequently with curiosity and anxiety.

In a way, this mobile is causing stress to everyone. When we send a message and if there is no response or reply or reaction instantly that creates stress. If we send a mail to someone and if they don't respond, that creates stress. When we call someone and if they don't answer our call, that creates stress. We are surrounded and bombarded by stress from all around every second and every minute of our life.

Technology has advanced a lot. With this Artificial Intelligence, digital era has entered in to a new phase.

We are always one choice
away from getting the best
and having the best. Those
who take that right choice at
every step will climb to the
top. Those who take wrong
choice at every step will
remain at average.
Right Choice Morning !!

PASSION PRASAD

Chapter 15

Physical Exercise

I am not writing this chapter on how to do physical exercise or how to improve your muscles. There is innumerable number of books, videos, classes on this subject.

But I just want to emphasize the importance of physical exercise in every day of our life. It is very crucial and vital for the success and progress in life. Lack of physical exercise will deprive of many good things in life.

Some people may not realize the importance of physical workout. They are busy with their careers or making money or other things. But they will regret in later part of their life that they should have done some physical workout when they were young.

MAN Changes, GAME changes is the essence of rituals. It is about what you get by what you do. If physical workout is lacking then the GAME will eventually fail. Even if they made money, it will eventually be of no good use as it has to be spent on hospital bills and medication.

In the academic education, the importance of physical exercise must be stressed in capital letters. There are some physical activities or sports or games in the schools, but there is no proper education on the importance of this, in particular.

If you want GAME to be better and brighter, MAN should be stricter and stronger.

If MAN is managed properly, GAME will be set proportionately.

If MAN is taken care of, GAME is well taken care of.

If MAN is perfect, we do not need hospitals.

If MAN is perfect, we do not need psychiatrists.

IF MAN is perfect, there will be peace and happiness in life.

IF MAN is not perfect, then all other challenges and problems may try to come up one by one in our lives.

If MAN is good, GAME is good.

Flash Thought:

The other day, I went to the hospital as I had some pain in my stomach. They did an ECG, X-ray, Blood Test, Urine Test, and Stool Test and said that I should go to a Gastric Specialist. When I went to him, he did an ultrasound and other tests and prescribed medicines. Apart from that, he referred me to a Psychiatrist. I was shocked at this. Why do I need to see a psychiatrist? Anyway, after making an appointment, one day, I went to the Psychiatrist, and they said we needed several sessions to explore the problem. Then, I went back to the gastro specialist, who referred me to a cardiologist for further tests.

I got fed up at this point. This all seems to be a vicious business cycle. They mention the name of a new technical term, and they refer to that specialist.

There may be a small problem, but I do not deny that. But these people try to make it complex and try to victimize the patient psychologically so that he will spend more money which is beneficial to the hospital.

I hope everyone realizes this fact and maintain their MAN properly, and then we do not need be afraid of all these new technical terms that can gradually minimize our bank balance.

I do agree that there are some genuine doctors and some decent hospitals where they diagnose properly to the point and give medications accordingly. But they are only a few. All the rest are money making institutions. Beware...

If MAN is proper, we don't need to go to hospitals.

***

No matter what happens, you will always find a way. There is no problem that is unsolved in this world. Just we need to seek for the solution. Right mindset gets you there.

Right Mindset Morning !!

PASSION PRASAD

Chapter 16

Miracles

Do you believe in Miracles? Yes, I do believe in miracles and they can happen in everyone's life. Miracles happen to those who believe. Miracles happen to those who trust. Miracles happen to those who have faith. Miracles happened in my life plenty of times. It can happen in your life too.

My definition of Miracles is as described below:

M - Money

I - Intellect

R - Romance

A - Abundance

C - Calmness

L - Love

E - Energy

S - Success

If you experience any of above things in your life, it is nothing but a miracle. The secret for miracles to happen is belief. If one is positive and optimistic, he can experience miracles. If one has hope and he believe in it, he can experience miracles. If one has determination, focus and hard work, he can experience miracles.

Again, experiencing miracles is a mindset. Being a millionaire is a mindset. Being healthy is a mindset. Being in a good relationship is a mindset. Getting creative ideas is a mindset. Being energetic is a mindset. Being romantic is a mindset. Being calm is a mindset. Being successful is a mindset. Being loved is a mindset. Being intelligent is a mindset. Overall, miracles are a mindset.

If we can tune our mindset to the frequency of the universe, miracles happen.

Human beings are creative creatures and creating creatures. Every moment, every hour, and every day, we create several things. Some create art, paintings, and songs, compose music, write articles and innovative ideas and some may sit idle and produce negative thoughts. But human beings can never sit quietly without doing anything. Positive or negative, constructive or destructive, profitable or not profitable, innovative or of no value, but something is being produced or created by everyone every minute.

If we want miracles in life, we need a different mindset. As the law of attraction states that, "Thoughts become things". By changing our thoughts, we can attract miracles in our life. I have experienced it personally in my life not once, but several times. It works.

We all know that the inspiration comes from within. Motivation always comes from external things by way of triggering. When motivation and inspiration join together, miracles happen. When miracles happen, innovations happen. It's like multiplier. Every good thing happens. Miracles itself is a good thing and miracles have magnetism and charisma. They attract lot of good things with them.

At this juncture I would like to mention that there is a word opposite to miracles and that word is chaos. Some people say there is a chaos in their life. When chaos is there miracles cannot happen. Miracles and chaos can never stay together. Where there are miracles there is no place for chaos and where there is chaos there is no place for miracles. This is guaranteed.

We can choose only one of them. That is possible by aligning our mindset positively or negatively. Positive mindset attracts miracles in life and negative mindset attracts chaos in life. It is as simple as that.

I wish there is a known as Mindset Monitor like a BP Monitor, Sugar Monitor, Thermometer etc. Such a device can instantly display whether we are in a positive state or a negative state. When our BP is high, we take medicines to bring it under control. When the sugar levels are high, we take medication to bring it under control. Similarly, when we know our state is negative, we can take certain measures to bring it to positive. I hope such devices can be invented with technological advancement.

But one more thought to add. We really don't need such a device. We always know whether we are positive or negative. If someone says that he doesn't know, then he is just pretending that's all. The people around us can easily tell whether we are positive or negative. The events happening in our lives can reveal whether we are positive or negative. Our surroundings and circumstances are nothing but a reflection of our inner positive or inner state. Now, do we need another device to monitor this?

When you live a life of abundance, miracles can happen in our life. But when we live a life of scarcity, then miracles have no chance in our life.

Flash Thought:

Whenever we travel by plane, in the airport and after immigration, our state of mind will be completely different. We feel very light and completely out of all stress and strain. I think everyone experiences this relaxed state after the immigration clearance. I guess this state is similar to the Alpha level in meditation. We are absolutely in a delighted state, and this state continues till we reach the destination airport. If the destination is a vacation, our serene state of mind continues. But if we reach back to our home town, our previous state resumes.

Airports really have a charm. We feel different energy in the airports. The beauty of the airports, the atmosphere, the lighting, the shopping, presence of different people of various cultures and costumes, the enthusiasm, the vibrancy of the place and all these things uplift our mood and we will be in an inspired and motivated state of mind. It paves way to get more creative and beautiful thoughts in that state of mind.

I love to travel as frequently as possible. In airports everyone wants to look pretty and handsome. Everyone tries to be energetic and that energy is contagious. I wish I can stay maximum time in the airports. We rarely see gloominess or dullness in the airports. Even those people who are in wheel chairs also smile and feel different energy. I love that....

***

Flash Thought:

Many people start things well, but some people's ending is not that good. Success is when anything is started well and ends well. We must make sure that the same energy continues from the beginning till the end. Energy loss will lead to total loss. Whether it is a project or a plan or a task or health or anything, energy should be strong.

Some athletes lose energy in the final leg, and they eventually lose to their competitors who have more energy. In fact, we should project and bring forth higher energy in the final moments to be victorious or successful.

Energy brings love. Energy brings good health. Energy brings all forms of wealth. Energy brings romance. Energy brings good relationships. Energy leads to success. Energy leads to miracles.

Feel the energy and miracles in your life.

***

Flash Thought:

Everyone has strengths and weaknesses. Everyone has some favourite things in their life. Similar way, everyone has some allergies in their life. Whenever we go to doctor, the nurse asks, "Do you have any allergy for any food or medicines"? Not only food or medicine, everyone will have some or other allergy in their life. Having allergy is not bad at all.

Some are allergic to sweets. Some are allergic to certain kind of vegetables. Some are allergic to certain kind of weather. Some are allergic to certain flavours. Some are allergic to certain perfumes. Some are allergic to certain kind of food. Some are allergic to certain medicines.

When we are allergic to something that thought or that thing or that object or that place or that person bring a different kind of feeling in our mind and heart. It's not a pleasant feeling. It can change our mood or can alter the state of our health and our cheerfulness.

Everyone should identify their allergies and try their best to avoid them and to take appropriate measures to prevent that kind of unpleasant feeling. Be away from allergies and be away from anxieties. This can be a best practice to keep one happy and peaceful.

Opportunities & Obstacles are
a bundle package. There is no
opportunity without obstacle
and no obstacle without
opportunity. Never look only
for opportunities and never be
afraid of obstacles. They go
hand in hand.
Opportunities Morning !!

PASSION PRASAD

Chapter 17

Be Authentic

In this cut, copy & paste modern world, try your best to be yourself. Try to be authentic. We are born different and born unique. When we live our life authentically, we will be honoured and we will have satisfaction.

All the people who received standing ovations are people who lived their authentic life. If we do not live authentic life, we will have no standing.

To live authentic life means being you. No need to imitate anyone else. You can emulate your ideal people, but still be yourself.

Being authentic is living your life with your passions, interests, and dreams with full energy and enthusiasm.

Being authentic is living your life and not living others' lives or others' dreams

Being authentic is not being influenced by others' interests and others' dreams

Flash Thought:

Everything is connected with three factors, person, time and place. These are three dimensions of human world. One's mood, energy, health, growth, prosperity, progress and all are dependent on the combination of two or more of these components.

A person is strong at a certain time. A person can be strong at a certain place. The same person can be much stronger at that particular place at that particular time. But the same person may not be so strong at a different time and at a different place.

For example, an individual is happy on his birthday. This is a combination of person and time. But if he wants to celebrate his birthday with his loved ones, which will make him much happier, this is a combination of person, place and time. That is much more powerful.

When one wants to propose to his or her friend, he will look for the right time and a right place. If he can make it at that time and at that place, it makes him extremely happy. This is the power of person, time and place.

Imagine someone wants to go for a vacation. When he buys a flight ticket to go to a certain destination, he will eagerly look forward to that date and time to catch up the flight. This is a combination of person and time. But when he reaches his destination that is a magical combination of person, time and place. That brings extreme delight.

When two people are going to get married, they look forward to the wedding date and time with utmost eagerness. That is a combination of person and time. But on that day, when they tie the knot or exchange the ring at the stipulated place, that is the magical moment. This is the combination of person, time and place.

Like in mathematics, there are x, y and z coordinates. Even in life, person, time, and place are three coordinates, the combination of which can be highly powerful and extremely productive.

That is why the name of the person, date of birth and place of birth are the key elements in any passport or identity card.

Imagine someone is going to graduate on a certain day, he or she will be anxiously looking forward to that date. Moreover, if he or she is going to attend the convocation on a certain date at a certain auditorium, it will be a historic moment in that person's life. This is a historic combination of person, time and place. A memory one will remember for all his life.

When we take a selfie or a picture with our friends, the picture contains the people, when it is taken and where it is taken. This is the magic of person, time and place, the three magic coordinates of human life.

Even when a person leaves this planet, on the tomb the name of the person, his year of birth and year of death will be written. When he is buried at a certain place, that person will be remembered for that date and place. His loved ones may visit him every year or sometime on that day at that particular place to offer prayers for his soul.

These all examples emphasize the importance of person, time and place. When we meet our friends after long time, the entire conversation will revolve around the friends, where they are and when they went there, which is nothing but person, place and time.

All the literature, history, books, episodes, stories,

movies and conversations basically connect these three coordinates to get the maximum information or excitement or entertainment or exploration.

I presume in future, there will be an invention of time machines which can get all the information or details when we enter one, or two, or three coordinates of any individual. I can imagine the time machine as a small cubical connected to a processing machine. If a person enters that cubicle, the face recognition and mentioned date and time can exactly show where that person was at that time. This machine may also be able to predict the future of what we will be doing at a particular time and place.

Always my imagination goes wild. I am imagining that this machine can help in decoding the crime scenes and can help in catching the criminals. Time machine can be a powerful device connecting the mysterious three coordinates of human past, present and future.

To be authentic, we need to be with authentic people. If we have wrong company or association with manipulative minds, it will have influence on our thoughts, character, behaviour and attitude. As a result, we too will become manipulative and can never reach authenticity.

Our association is of prime importance in being authentic, in being successful and in being productive. We are what our peers are. As we always hear the word "peer pressure", we are always influenced by the people around us. Change the people around you and change your destiny. It's as simple as that.

The entire personal development guru's recommending to join Master Mind Groups. It's always effective, productive and profitable. There is a magic when you are with likeminded people. Everyone in the group resonate the same frequency and vibration. We aspire for greater results with optimum efficiency and synergy. Master Mind groups are very much effective.

When great minds join together, great things happen. When amazing things happen, they inspire everyone. When all are energized, much greater things can happen. This is the power of energy and synergy.

Flash Thought:

Elderly people have lot of knowledge because of their extensive experience. They have lot of wisdom to share. Whenever they meet people they have lot of stories to tell. Sometimes few people neglect elderly people and they don't want to listen to their stories.

But elderly people need attention. They need our time. They need our hearing ear. By spending time with them, we can make them happy, and at the same time, we can gain more knowledge.

If we have elderly parents or grandparents at home, we need to allocate some time for them every day in spite of our busy schedules. The house where elderly people are respected and treated well will be blessed. The community where elderly people are happy will be flourishing multi-fold.

Love can conquer anything.
Patience can win everything.
Will power can achieve
anything. Determination can
defeat everything. Focus
can capture anything.
Anything Possible Morning !!

PASSION PRASAD

Chapter 18

Conclusion

Are you convinced that MAN Changes, GAME Changes?

I am crystal clear that this will work. By realigning our rituals, we can reach our GAME effectively, efficiently and more accurately.

Our rituals can predict our future. Our rituals can predict our destiny. Our destiny is in our rituals. Follow the best practices and get the best results. This is simple success formula.

I thoroughly enjoyed my journey of writing this book. This concept started in my mind around ten years ago. But I did not take any steps after that. Recently, I met Dr Kailash Pinjani (not by accident, but by coincidence), and then it took shape. As always, the Universe will always conspire to make you successful. Things will happen in the right direction. You will meet the right people. You will face the right opportunities. You just need to align your energy and focus on your goals. It will be manifested under all circumstances.

Thanks to Dr Kailash.

Through Dr Kailash, I met Dr Deepak Parbat, who is the main man behind the publishing of this book. His ideas, tips and suggestions added beauty to the look of this whole book. Many, many thanks to Dr Deepak.

I sincerely pray that each and every one on earth should live peacefully with joy and grow exponentially in knowledge and their wisdom. By reading this book our souls are connected even though we have not met physically. My ardent prayers are with you all. Let's strive to make this planet a better place for everyone and even for future generations. Let peace prevail everywhere!!

Ask yourself:
What can I do to achieve my dream ?
What shall I do to achieve my dream?
What should I do to achieve my dream?
What must I do to achieve my dream?
Please write down...
Action Morning !!

PASSION PRASAD

Smile & Shine
Passion Prasad

About the Author

- Certified Leadership Challenge Facilitator

- Certified Passion Test Facilitator

- Certified Law of Attraction Facilitator

- Trained in UK & USA by Chris Attwood & Janet Attwood (Authors of New York's Best-Selling Book "The Passion Test"

- Certified NLP Practitioner directly from Richard Bandler

- Participated in "Unleash The Power Within" by Tony Robbins

- Participated in "Millionaire Mind Intensive" by T. Harv Eker

- Participated in "7 Habits of Highly Effective people" by Steven Covey

- Certified Practitioner of MBTI

- 7 Years' Experience as Sales & Marketing Manager at Jumbo Electronics (LG) in Qatar

- 20+ Years of total experience in Sales & Marketing in India, Saudi Arabia, Malaysia, Qatar & UAE

- Past President of Talking Matters Toastmasters Club in Qatar

- Past Director of BNI Pioneer Chapter in Qatar

TVS PRASAD

(Passion Prasad)

Trainer, Coach & Facilitator

Ph: 00971 525441274, U.A.E.

prasad@passionprasad.com

Forget and forgive. If we have not forgotten some unwanted things, we have not grown. If we don't forgive someone who did hurt us, we have not matured. Forget and forgive shows that we have evolved. Forget & Forgive Morning!!

PASSION PRASAD

About The Book

"MAN Changes, GAME Changes" is a single window solution to everyone's everyday challenges, dreams and their aspirations. If the reader can understand, analyse and implement the tips and techniques offered in this book, his or her GAME can really change.

We wish every reader should have pleasant feelings and experience while their expedition to the portals of this book. We wish every reader a pleasant reading….

Anything worth doing is worth waiting. Sometimes real good things take their own time and we should let it take it's own process. If it's worth having, it's worth waiting. Don't rush.
Worth Waiting Morning !!

PASSION PRASAD

If you wish to subscribe for Daily Motivational Messages, please send your whatsapp number to prasad@passionprasad.com

---

If you wish to send your comments / feedback about this book, please send an email to prasad@passionprasad.com